Your Happy Healthy Pet™

Hamster

2nd Edition

Betsy Sikora Siino

Wiley Publishing, Inc.

This book is printed on acid-free paper.

Howell Book House
Published by Wiley Publishing, Inc., Hoboken, New Jersey

For general information on our other products and services or to obtain technical support please contact our Customer Care Department within the U.S. at (800) 762-2974, outside the U.S. at (317) 572-3993 or fax (317) 572-4002.

Wiley also publishes its books in a variety of electronic formats. Some content that appears in print may not be available in electronic books. For more information about Wiley products, please visit our web site at www.wiley.com.

Library of Congress Cataloging-in-Publication Data:
Siino, Betsy Sikora.
Hamster / Betsy Sikora Siino.—2nd ed.
p. cm.—(Your happy healthy pet)
ISBN-13 978-0-470-03793-5 (cloth: alk. pap
ISBN-10 0-470-03793-8 (cloth: alk. paper)
1. Hamsters as pets. I. Title. II. Series.
SF459.H3S53 2007
636.935'6—dc22
Printed in the United States of America

10 9 8 7 6 5 4 3 2 1

2nd Edition

Book design by Melissa Auciello-Brogan
Cover design by Michael J. Freeland
Book production by Wiley Publishing, Inc. Composition Services

About the Author

Betsy Sikora Siino is an award-winning author who has written hundreds of articles and more than two dozen books on animals and their care. She is a former staff writer and features editor for several national pet publications, including *Dog Fancy, Horse Illustrated,* and *Pet Health News.* Her books include *The Complete Idiot's Guide to Choosing a Pet,* books on a variety of dog and horse breeds, *You Want a What for Pet?!,* and *For the Life of Your Dog* (written with Olympic Gold Medalist Greg Louganis). One of Betsy's greatest pleasures through the years has been seeing pet owners and prospective pet owners, adults and children alike, seek sound information on the proper care of animals—even small pocket pets like the hamster.

About Howell Book House

Since 1961, Howell Book House has been America's premier publisher of pet books. We're dedicated to companion animals and the people who love them, and our books reflect that commitment. Our stable of authors—training experts, veterinarians, breeders, and other authorities—is second to none. And we've won more Maxwell Awards from the Dog Writers Association of America than any other publisher.

As we head toward the half-century mark, we're more committed than ever to providing new and innovative books, along with the classics our readers have grown to love. This year, we're launching several exciting new initiatives, including redesigning the Howell Book House logo and revamping our biggest pet series, Your Happy Healthy Pet™, with bold new covers and updated content. From bringing home a new puppy to competing in advanced equestrian events, Howell has the titles that keep animal lovers coming back again and again.

Contents

Shopping List

You'll need to prepare your new pet's home and stock up on supplies before you bring your hamster home. Below is a basic list of some must-have supplies. For more detailed information on selecting each of these items, consult chapter 4. Remember, too, that you will need to buy items that are the right size for whatever type of hamster you have chosen.

- ☐ Cage or tank
- ☐ Various nest boxes
- ☐ Food bowl
- ☐ Water bottle with metal sipping tube
- ☐ Hamster food
- ☐ Safe bedding (no cedar or pine, please!)
- ☐ Chewing materials
- ☐ Pet carrier or travel cage
- ☐ Hamster wheel
- ☐ Soft brush or toothbrush
- ☐ Safe toys

There are likely to be a few other items that you're dying to pick up before bringing your hamster home. Use the following blanks to note any additional items you'll be shopping for.

- ☐ ______________________________
- ☐ ______________________________
- ☐ ______________________________
- ☐ ______________________________
- ☐ ______________________________
- ☐ ______________________________
- ☐ ______________________________
- ☐ ______________________________
- ☐ ______________________________
- ☐ ______________________________
- ☐ ______________________________

Pet Sitter's Guide

We can be reached at (___)_____-________ Cellphone (___)_____-________

____

We will return on ____________ (date) at ____________ (approximate time)

Hamster's Name ______________________________

Breed, Age, and Sex __________________________

Important Names and Numbers

Vet's Name ________________________ Phone (___)_____-________

Address ____________________________________

Emergency Vet's Name ________________ Phone (___)_____-________

Address ____________________________________

Poison Control ________________________ (or call vet first)

Other individual to contact in case of emergency ________________

____

Care Instructions

In the following blanks, let the sitter know what to feed, how much, and when; when to offer out-of-cage time; when to give treats; and explain cage cleaning requirements.

Morning ____________________________________

____

Evening ____________________________________

____

____

Any special medical needs ____________________

____

Grooming instructions ________________________

____

Cage cleaning instructions ____________________

____

My hamster's favorite playtime activities, quirks, and other tips ___________

____

____

Part I
The World of the Hamster

The Hamster

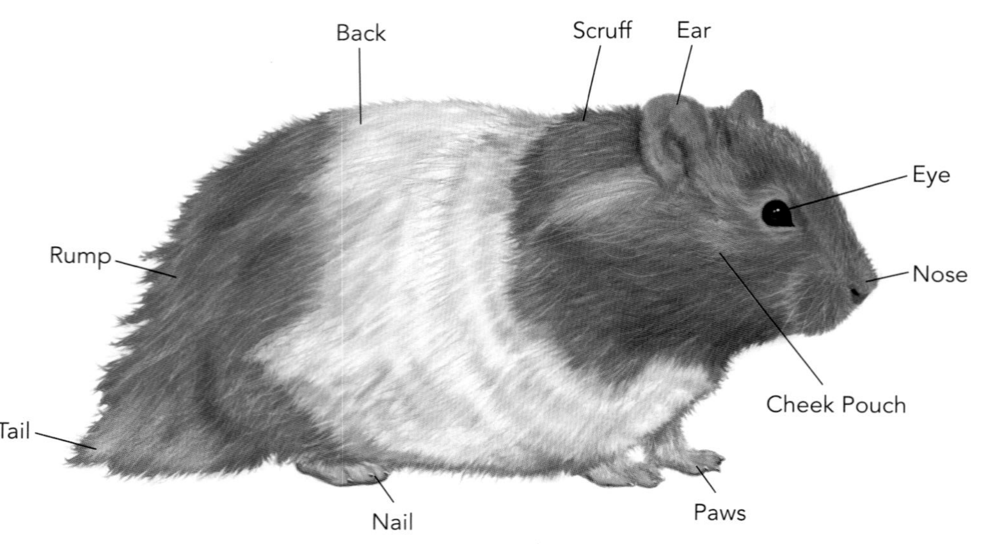

Chapter 1

What Is a Hamster?

Imagine a friend who is soft and warm and fits in the palm of your hand. A gentle soul, he is most content among those who respect his quiet nature, his diminutive size, and his unique view of the world. He's fundamentally a vegetarian (though he might say yes to a bite of meat now and again, if it's offered) who demands a clean home and regular exercise, yet he tends to be a bit too susceptible to stress. Though a homebody at heart, he can also be an inquisitive guy with a desire to explore the world beyond his cage door. Much to his benefit, as we will see, he also doesn't happen to have much of a tail.

The little friend of whom we speak is, of course, the hamster. And when you gather together all his special characteristics, you can't help but see that there is far more to him than meets our human eyes.

A Misunderstood Family

Many among us believe we know what hamsters are. After all, what is there to know? They're just those little animals that you put in a cage and keep in the kids' room. They're pretty easy to take care of, and they like to run on those wheels. Not much to it.

But if he had the voice and the language skills, the hamster would be the first to tell us that he is far too often misunderstood—even underestimated—by the two-legged creatures who call themselves his caretakers. He would be the first to tell us that although living with humans is a fine fate for his kind, he would be even more comfortable if people would take a little time to get to know him before welcoming him into their homes. Perhaps then, even though he enjoys immense popularity, he might earn a little more respect as well.

Answering the Question

The first step toward increasing our understanding of hamsters is to explore their family tree. But here, too, some misunderstandings might arise. The most logical answer to the question "What is a hamster?," you see, also happens to be the simplest answer. A hamster is a rodent. That's what he is.

Uh oh.

Many a would-be hamster owner may not be all that pleased to hear that answer. When we think *rodent,* we think of mice in the kitchen cupboard munching the Cheerios or rats in the garbage can scavenging for Thanksgiving leftovers. We don't tend to think of a soft, cuddly companion sharing our children's bedrooms. But to leap to such unsavory conclusions is to underestimate what is, in truth, a fascinating, even amazing, branch of the animal kingdom that has lived closely with humans throughout much of our history. Frankly, that fact alone deserves our respect.

So our first step toward understanding the hamster the way he would like us to understand him is to explore his extended family, his roots: the family of rodents.

The Rodent Clan

In the vast sea of species that comprise the animal kingdom, the hamster is a member of the rodent order of mammals. The rodents, in fact, are the largest of all mammalian orders. Approximately 50 percent of all mammalian species are

Our relationship with rodents has not always been friendly, partly because they like to eat the grain we store.

rodents, and, thanks to the phenomenal adaptability of these animals, almost all of those species are quite large and healthy in number.

Rodents are essentially named for their world-class gnawing abilities. The word "rodent" comes from the Latin word *rodere*, which means to gnaw. Rodents are able to gnaw so effectively because their teeth are designed for a special style of jaw movement that has ensured their survival through the ages. They have one pair of upper and one pair of lower incisor teeth. Both pairs grow constantly throughout the animal's life and require regular gnawing activity to remain trimmed to a manageable length.

In terms of physical characteristics, most rodent species are relatively small and compact. They use their delicate "hands" to carry out a variety of functions, including collecting and manipulating food, and grooming. Some rodents, such as the hamster, are also graced with ample cheek pouches, in which they can store large amounts of food to carry to secret caches, where they can store the food for a time when food is not so plentiful.

Rodents' teeth, combined with the various species' evolutionary gifts (which typically include staggering reproduction rates), and their uncanny ability to reap the benefits of close proximity to humans, have led these animals to be regarded almost exclusively as pests (particularly rodents of the rat and mice varieties). But let's give credit where it's due. Theirs is an amazing family of animals found all over the globe in all geographical regions and climates.

Pest or Companion? You Be the Judge

We humans have collected a great deal of information about the various species of rodents, because, much to our chagrin, where there are humans, there are probably very opportunistic rodents close by. The two cannot be separated. That is simply a fact of life and always has been.

Rodents are smart critters who learned long ago that it was much to their benefit to live in close proximity to humans—a testament to rodent adaptability and even intelligence. Once humans made their grand entrance within the animal kingdom, many other animal species realized that where there are humans, there is food and shelter, too. As human populations have spread across the globe, they have invariably overtaken lands that were originally occupied by nonhuman species—or inadvertently transported those species with them. Many of these species have not survived our encroachment or their own immigration, but others have, and with great success. Case in point: the rodents.

Given their proximity to humans, it is to the family's misfortune that rodents have also come to be known as carriers of disease and parasites, thanks primarily to the fleas they carried that led to the spread of the plague throughout Europe during the Middle Ages. Because of this guilt by association, to this day the possibility of a rodent invading our food supply, home, and/or workplace has caused humans great concern. When we see the first telltale sign of a gnawed cardboard box in the pantry, we panic, sterilize our homes, and start setting out poison and traps. Of course, in many cases all we really need to do is think ahead and work to prevent these uninvited guests from entering our homes in the first place by storing our food correctly in secure, airtight containers.

And yet, it seems that various rodents—including the hamster, and even the mouse and the rat—have had the last laugh, as they have become domesticated household companions to humans. Here we humans are, feeding them, sheltering them, and in some cases even buying them toys and helping them increase their numbers by breeding them purposely. Perhaps these animals have much more in the brain department than we give them credit for.

What Makes a Hamster a Rodent?

As we already know, a hamster is part of the rodent order of mammals. They are covered with fur, are warm-blooded, and give birth to live young. Much to these animals' great benefit, with few exceptions, hamsters have only the tiniest stub of a tail. This makes them more acceptable as pets to people who are haunted by images of rats, regarded with such disgust by many for their long, naked tails.

Let's explore a little further how rodent characteristics manifest in the members of the large extended family that we call hamsters. The more you can learn about these traits, the better equipped you will be to provide your hamster with all he needs for the healthiest, most satisfying, longest life possible.

LaFawndah shows off her rodent teeth.

The Teeth

We can always tell a rodent by his teeth. While the various rodent species are typically recognized by their differences in color, size, coat type, tail, behavior, sleeping habits, social structure, and dietary preferences, all share a common characteristic in their front teeth, their incisors. Take a look at any hamster, especially at mealtime as he carefully nibbles a tasty morsel of food held in his delicate grasp, and you'll see clearly the miracles that are rodent teeth.

The rodent incisors are marvels of engineering that continue to grow throughout the individual rodent's life. The jaw is structured to ensure that the animal can constantly gnaw, to keep his chisel-like incisors properly filed.

This gnawing action also enables those incisors to contact the lower set of teeth at just the right angle to finish the job. Marvels of engineering are not typically what most of us think of when we think of hamsters, but there they are.

If the hamster's ever-growing incisors are not properly filed in the course of his day-to-day activities—which will happen to the unfortunate rodent with a misaligned jaw—the animal will starve to death and suffer a great deal of pain in the meantime, as his teeth continue to grow and pierce various regions of his mouth and face.

The Hip Glands

The typical hamster has two large glands on each side of his body, close to his hips. Males have larger glands than those we find on female hamsters. The glands secrete an oily substance that acts as a territory marker (perhaps an issue more important to the males of the species). The hamster's fur usually hides the glands, but sometimes a wet spot or matted fur will indicate their location on the hamster's body.

You may sometimes spot your hamster rubbing up against the sides of his cage or enclosure; this is an instinctive, territorial behavior. Hamsters in the wild, you see, rub themselves against the walls of their burrows to mark their presence and stake their territory. Hamsters have a mild musk scent that can sometimes be detected when their glands are actively secreting. Because their eyesight is not typically their strongest sense, hamsters rely upon these scent markings to designate and recognize their territory.

Rodent Reproduction

To ensure that their species survive through all eternity, especially when confronted daily by pest-extermination companies and successful predator species ranging from foxes to coyotes to bears to humans, rodents are phenomenally quick breeders. They need to make sure that even if many, many individuals die, their species will survive.

This characteristic is one shared by the hamster members of the rodent family—which comes as no surprise to those unsuspecting owners who didn't realize they had a male and female in that cage rather than the two females the pet-shop clerk promised.

Most hamsters reach sexual maturity within a few weeks after birth, and, if left to their own devices, they will begin reproducing at the first opportunity. They often produce large litters, and may find themselves caring for two or three generations just weeks apart in age.

Types of Hamsters

As we can see, hamsters embody the classic characteristics of their extended rodent family. For some reason, however, we have decided to designate them as pet rather than pest. As a result, we have seen the hamster family grow in type as well as numbers, often with the determined and very calculated assistance of humans.

Today, hamsters who have forged long-term relationships with humans come in all sizes, colors, personalities, and geographical preferences. So before one simply lumps all hamsters under a single name and assumes that all are identical in behavior and lifestyle, it is wise to take a look into the world of these animals and see what differences exist between the various hamsters.

The Classic Golden (a.k.a. Syrian)

The most well known of all the hamster species, the one most commonly kept as a household pet, is the golden, or Syrian, hamster. When parents regale their children with loving stories about their own childhood hamster, an animal with

Esther is a classic golden hamster.

Classic Golden Facts

Classic golden hamsters are usually about 6 to 8 inches long (although they can grow as big as 11 inches) and weigh 3 to 5 ounces. They are thought to be colorblind and probably see their world in shades of black and white. Typically nocturnal by nature (but, in keeping with their rodent roots, somewhat adaptable to the daytime schedules in their human households), golden hamsters are most active in the hours between 7 and 11 p.m.

whom they bonded and learned to appreciate as a unique individual, that hamster was probably a golden.

As his name suggests, the classic golden hamster is gold: typically, gold on his back with white on his underside (a pattern that is perhaps designed to camouflage the animal in his desert homeland), with large, dark eyes that help him navigate the terrain during his nocturnal forays. But in light of the popularity of this attractive pocket pet, humans have selectively bred the golden to alter what nature made. This has resulted in vast differences of appearances within the species.

Technically, there is only one species of pet golden. But, thanks to careful breeding practices, there are now a number of varieties. Colors abound, including cinnamon, cream, white, black, silver, and more. Purists believe the original golden remains the most genetically healthy, because the colors are often produced by breeding related individuals. Coat patterns abound as well, evident in the spots and patches seen on so many contemporary hamsters. But of course, one would never find such patterns on hamsters in the wild.

Also absent in the wild are longhaired hamsters or those with short, soft, velvety coats. Yet pet hamsters with these characteristics do exist in captivity today, thanks to breeding practices that encourage the long hair of the so-called teddy bear hamster, and the shiny, velvety texture of the satin, both of which have become quite popular pets. There are also longhaired and shorthaired rex hamsters, whose coats are wavy and tend to stand out from the animals' bodies. Rex hamsters also have curly whiskers. And finally, breeders have even produced hairless hamsters with nothing but curly whiskers.

Bring on the Dwarfs

While the golden may be the classic, there is a new kid on the block who is taking the hamster world by storm. Actually, make that several new kids. These are the various dwarf hamsters, adorable little critters who are becoming more and more popular in hamster-owning homes nationwide.

A relative newcomer to captivity, the dwarf thus far seems to be taking to life among humans quite well, earning positive reviews as a family pet. Dwarf hamsters can range in length from 2 to 4 inches. There are several dwarf species, identified by their small size, delicate feet, and compact, ball-like physique, as well as their desire to live with others of their kind—an arrangement the solitary golden hamster simply cannot tolerate. Most of them are quite beautiful in addition to their "cute" factor.

While some owners say dwarfs are more prone than goldens to bite the hands that feed them, others enjoy the fact that dwarfs, who may be more challenging to tame, tend to be more sociable with others of their own kind. Their fans do tend to claim, however, that dwarf hamsters can be quite docile and friendly with the humans in their lives, if those humans are willing to maintain regular socialization practices and handle them very gently. But such endorsements must be tempered with the warning that hamster congeniality usually has more to do with an individual hamster than with the species at large. And always, it is rooted in positive experiences with humans and other hamsters, and positive associations forged from being handled gently and socialized carefully from a young age.

Koutouzis is a Russian dwarf hamster.

The Russians

In the early 1900s, a gentleman named W. C. Campbell discovered a unique and very tiny hamster who would go on to immortalize his name. Today the Campbell's, or Russian, dwarf is probably the most popular dwarf hamster on the pet market. The dwarf we call the Russian hails not only from Russia, but also from China and Mongolia, and his popularity derives from his soft coat, the dorsal stripe that runs down his back, his small size, his round physique, and all the attributes that have led to the popularity of dwarfs in the first place.

As happens with any hamster who enjoys popularity, the Campbell's Russian is found in many color variations and usually has a sleek, shiny coat, similar to that of the Syrian hamster.

The Campbell's Russian is not, however, the only Russian dwarf out there. The winter white dwarf, also know as the Siberian dwarf, is similar to the Campbell's, but, as he would be the first to tell you, is not the same. He is the smaller of the two Russians, and he is called winter white because if kept in a cool environment, his typically gray coat can turn pure white. He is also known to be amiable and relatively easy to hand tame.

The Roborovski Dwarf

Another type of dwarf hamster you are more and more likely to find these days is the Roborovski dwarf. He is the smallest of the dwarfs. He is also the dwarf most likely to win sprint medals at the Olympics because he tends to be the fastest. Keep this in mind when you are choosing his home (a glass aquarium tank is probably a better choice than a traditional cage). You'll also need an extra-safe security plan when you would like to spend time with him outside his habitat.

If you ever need to identify an escaped Roborovski, you can recognize him by his white eyebrows and his lack of the dorsal stripe made popular by his Russian cousins.

The Chinese Dwarf

To the untrained eye, this dwarf hamster may resemble a mouse, the primary reason for this being the presence of a tail. He is usually found in one of two color variations: brown with a white stripe down the back and a white stomach, or white with brown patches. The Chinese hamster's body type tends to be long and thin, and his personality depends largely on how he is tamed as a youngster.

Zippy is a Chinese dwarf hamster.

You may not quite know what you are getting with a Chinese hamster. Some are quite friendly, others . . . well . . . not so much. So it is essential that you look for breeders who hand tame their babies. This is not as difficult as it once was, because the Chinese dwarf is not nearly as rare on the American pet market as it was when dwarfs were first making a name for themselves as pets.

Wild Hamsters

With many rodent species that are typically kept as pets, you can sometimes choose between domestically bred animals and those who are captured in the wild and sold as pets. This is not the case with the hamster. Pet hamsters have been bred to be pets, pure and simple. However, there is one wild type of hamster who has quite a bit of experience with humans—most of it negative. This is the largest member of the hamster family, the common hamster, and he is not one you are likely to find as a pet. He is the only hamster seen readily in the wild today—although, unfortunately, not quite as readily as he once was.

A striking animal with an almost raccoon-like coat of black and brown, the common hamster is quite large for a hamster. This animal was once abundant throughout Russia and Central Europe, but his preference for a vegetarian diet proved to be his population's undoing. Naturally drawn to the crops cultivated on farms, the common hamster was targeted, as so many rodents are, as an enemy of farmers. The result has been a severe decline in the numbers of common hamsters in their native territory. Although common hamsters are not as plentiful in the wild as they once were, humanity discovered long ago that totally eliminating rodent populations is nearly impossible.

Periodically, there is talk of recruiting the common hamster into the ranks of pet hamsters, where he would join the golden and the dwarf. To date, that seems highly unlikely, given the common hamster's somewhat irritable and classically wild temperament when forced into captivity. Nevertheless, he remains an object of fascination to pet hamster enthusiasts. The common hamster embodies the typical hamster characteristics to which hamster owners have become accustomed—plus, as a bonus, he has a talent for swimming.

Other wild hamsters that are not typically kept as pets include various hamsters who live in Africa, Asia, and Western Europe. Some of these animals even have tails. These include Chinese hamsters, native not only to China, but to Europe and Russia as well; mouselike hamsters, who call the Middle East home; and white-tailed hamsters, native to South Africa and commonly referred to as the white-tailed rat. Like their cousin the common hamster, these species do not have the temperament or the physical adaptability to thrive in a captive environment with humans.

Chapter 2

Hamster History

Let's face it: We tend to take the hamster for granted. She is just a little pet who lives in many a child's bedroom as that all-important "first pet," and in countless school classrooms across the country, right?

Well, yes. Sometimes.

Take a closer look, though, and you'll find an animal with a history and a character that will explain perfectly why she has captivated generations of humans for so many years. And why her popularity is in no danger of diminishing any time soon.

The Source

Imagine if you will a vast forest, home for centuries to a complex, interconnected ecosystem of birds, mammals, fish, insects, and plants. Now imagine that forest is razed for cattle grazing or stripped for the building of tract homes. Just where do those animals go?

Those species that cannot adapt to human encroachment on their habitats are doomed either to displacement because of the loss of their food supplies and living space, or to outright destruction. To their credit, many rodents, even those targeted vigorously for destruction by humans, have actually benefited from human activity. While people who do not care to coexist with mice, rats, and their brethren may not be impressed by this fact, even they must admire how nature has enabled these rodent survivors to persist so efficiently.

Diet has also played a key role in rodent survival. Their physiological makeup permits most rodents to thrive on a variety of foods, thus ensuring that even when their favored or traditional dietary items disappear, there are always alternatives available. Most rodents can survive on a veritable smorgasbord of options, including vegetarian fare or foods of animal origin, including insects and worms.

Now that you understand just where hamsters come from and why they have survived, read on and you may discover why we love them the way we do.

The Evolution of Hamsters

As a card-carrying member of the rodent family, the hamster has been ever-nimble in her ability to deal with the elements, resulting in the evolution of a large and impressive band of hamster species. Within the rodent order, there are several suborders; the hamster is a member of the suborder *Myomorpha,* the mouselike rodents. This group includes the various hamster species, ranging in size from the tiny dwarfs that measure only 2 to 4 inches in length to the fascinating common hamster, the granddaddy of the family, who may reach lengths of 8 to 11 inches, to the ever-popular golden hamster who is somewhere between the two in size.

Hamsters, in general, are adaptable creatures, and were once found in a variety of regions, from mountains, to deserts, to agricultural fields. The classic golden, or Syrian, hamster (the one we typically think of when we think of hamster pets), is a desert rodent who evolved into twenty-four different known species of hamsters; only a few of these are kept as pets.

Because wild hamsters like to burrow underground to escape the heat and predators, we know very little about how they live their lives.

While a great deal is known and understood about rodent biology and sociology, until recently our pet hamster species remained somewhat elusive members of that family tree because of their wild ancestors' solitary, secretive lifestyles. Indeed, as is true of all rodent pets, the hamster's true beginnings are found in the wild. Yet because of this wild individual's tendency to burrow and spend a great deal of time underground, she was able to shield herself for thousands of years from prying humans who would seek to discover her secrets. Her cover finally blown within the last couple of hundred years, the hamster is today a relative newcomer to the roster of known animal species in general, and pets in particular.

Hamster Character

Perhaps because today so many hamsters live with us humans, we have learned quite a bit about them in a relatively short period of time. Yet we still don't take them very seriously. It is considered a joke when a hamster is cast as a mean and vicious villain in a child's horror story. And remember the comic strip *Calvin & Hobbes*? Calvin, the precocious 6-year-old, pleads with his harried dad to read him his favorite book over and over—one with a protagonist who just happens to be a hamster.

A hamster? What could be so interesting, so captivating about a hamster? Hamster enthusiasts, however, know that this humble, unassuming animal has plenty within her bag of magic tricks to captivate and charm us. They understand, as well, that her role as clever villain and fascinating children's hero is downright deserved. Get to know the hamster, and you will discover a fascinating creature who has mastered the superhero habits of a small animal forced to survive in treacherous wild environs—an animal who is equally adept at adapting those characteristics to life in captivity.

Of course, the hamster's physical and behavioral characteristics have been molded through the ages by her native home—the desert and other arid, often treacherous, extreme environs. Understand the link between the hamster's home territory and the appearance, behavior, and character of the contemporary pet hamster within your home, and you will be better able to enjoy your pet. You will also be better prepared to offer her the optimum care required to keep her spry and healthy until the ripe old age of 2 or 3 years.

Native Territory

In the golden hamster's ancient homeland, the daytime temperatures were generally warm, the night temperatures cool. Food was intermittently scarce and abundant. There was little vegetation and few landscape features to safely conceal a

A hamster's large eyes and ears help her navigate at night.

tiny rodent from predators. Now envision a quiet, gentle animal—the hamster—in the midst of such a scene, and think about how the characteristics of her native territory relate to the hamster's evolution.

From a physical perspective, here is a small rodent whose large, expressive eyes offer the first clue to how this animal would live in the wild. A nocturnal creature requires large eyes to see effectively in the dark. In the wild, she spends most of her waking hours under the cover of night, waiting until the atmosphere cools to seek her dinner.

The hamster's prominent ears also have a story to tell. They are positioned high on the animal's head so the hamster can best take advantage of her acute sense of hearing, especially when faced with the challenge of detecting the presence of an approaching predator—or the voice of a trusted owner.

The ample cheek pouches are another factor in the survival of the hamster. The hamster can stuff her pouches with almost half her body weight in food. The food may then be carried off and hidden in private caches for another day when food is not so plentiful (a habit pet hamsters may practice in captivity, as well). This would certainly explain why this animal's name is derived from the German word *hamstern*, meaning "to hoard."

As far as hamster behavior is concerned, not much is known about the hamster's life in the wild, and apparently that is precisely how the hamster has intended it to be. The golden hamster remained unknown for so long (and her natural, wild existence still remains something of a mystery) because of her rather mysterious lifestyle.

Natural Burrowers

Although details about her existence in the wild remain somewhat elusive, we do know that our pet hamster's wild counterpart spends her time primarily underground. A consummate burrower, the wild hamster passes her days beneath the surface of the earth, hiding in the cool catacombs of tunnels, safe from the harsh rays of the sun, the extreme temperatures, and the teeth and claws of rodent-hungry predators. She emerges from her safe, cool sanctuary when the sun sets to scavenge for her dinner.

Food is scarce in the hamster's native territory, a condition that subsequently served to mold our pet hamster into an animal who requires a great deal of exercise. In the wild, this small animal is forced to travel vast distances to find sustenance. Joke as we might about hamsters running aimlessly on their exercise wheels—miles and miles in a single day—the hamster is driven by instinct to a life of activity. Her very survival once depended on it.

We need to understand further that pet hamsters will live longer and more contentedly if they are provided with appropriate and varied opportunities to play and interact with people. This means making far more of an effort than simply supplying the animal with twenty-four-hour access to an exercise wheel, to which the hamster can become addicted, not to mention exhausted and dehydrated. The hamster's potential to thrive in the company of humans shows

From Desert Beginnings

Did you know that your fuzzy pet—queen of her Habitrail—once roamed the desert in a similarly complex networks of tunnels? The hamster has evolved for survival in a hostile desert environment, known for extreme temperatures, a lack of shelter, and a periodic scarcity of food. It's little wonder, then, that she took so readily to living with humans, discovering that if those humans are properly trained, the food is plentiful, the bedding is clean, and, we would hope, the caretakers are gentle and respectful.

us that perhaps even when living happily in that burrowed desert den, the wild hamster perhaps knew that she just might be missing something.

A Revolutionary Discovery

The hamster has come a long way from her existence as a golden shorthaired rodent in the wild to a popular pet who comes in many colors and coat types and lives within our homes. The events that would lead to the rise of the pet hamster began in 1829, when one of these small animals was discovered near the Syrian city of Aleppo by British zoologist George Waterhouse. He called this little rodent *Cricetus auratus*, or golden hamster, and she went on to enjoy a brief period of popularity as a pet, primarily in Britain. But despite this species' prolific breeding habits, the novelty of owning small, unique, mostly tailless rodents soon disappeared, as did the existence of hamsters in captivity.

Yet the hamster would not remain unknown forever. In 1930 a zoologist named Israel Aharoni, from Hebrew University in Jerusalem, found a female hamster and her litter of twelve while conducting research in the Syrian desert. He was, in fact, looking for these animals, inspired by historical accounts he had read that described quiet, docile animals known as Syrian mice, who were thought to have been kept as pets by the ancient Assyrians. When the zoologist discovered a small family of hamsters huddled in an underground burrow in the desert, he assumed that these were the so-called mice about which he had read.

While finding a family of rodents out in the desert would not, at first, seem to be earth-shattering, this particular discovery came as quite a surprise to those who knew rodents. Few had ever heard of the elusive hamster, and most of them assumed that because nobody had seen one in the past hundred years or so, the hamster species was extinct, both in the wild and in captivity. But the hamster had remained unseen, not because of a decline in her population (extinction is, for all practical purposes, a foreign concept to rodents), but because her secret, solitary nature and nocturnal habits had made it so. Now, her secret was out.

Jerusalem or Bust

Aharoni took his newly discovered hamster family to Jerusalem. Because so little was known about their care at the time, sadly, only three of them survived. A successful breeding program was launched with those remaining survivors, however, and today, thanks to that legendary reproductive potency for which rodents are known, each and every contemporary pet golden hamster is thought to be the direct offspring of those surviving three.

Hamsters like to hide—sometimes just for fun.

Having survived adversity (in keeping with their rodent heritage), these early captive-bred hamsters enjoyed a surge in numbers and in popularity. Word spread among those fortunate souls who came to know these unique little animals, and people found themselves naturally charmed. Nevertheless, those early hamsters and their progeny did not immediately take the pet world by storm. The species would first need to take a slight detour.

The Road to Domesticity

Once in the care of humans, hamsters were enlisted as laboratory animals—an unpleasant fate, to be sure, but one that taught people a great deal about how to keep these animals healthy in captivity. This information would later prove vital to the success of keeping hamsters as pets.

Today, hamsters continue to be used as lab animals, although the numbers of hamsters used for this purpose have declined substantially in the past twenty years or so. From the sterile halls of the laboratory environment, the hamster's reputation as a quiet, gentle animal (attributes that made her a desirable laboratory animal in the first place) spread. Hardly a surprise to those who had come to know her, the hamster soon found herself being targeted for a far more pleasant fate: family pet.

The hamster proved to be a natural at this calling, of course, and has blossomed within that friendly niche ever since. This great popularity is significant, considering that the hamster was officially "discovered" and enlisted into a partnership with humans only a few decades ago. That she has become such a common household pet in such a relatively short period of time is a testament to her charm and to her ideal characteristics as a pet.

Hamsters in the Classroom

An offshoot of the hamster's life as pet is the calling of "class pet." Unfortunately, though, this can be a dual-edged sword. The lucky class hamster is one in the care of a teacher who is skilled in and knowledgeable about the proper care and handling of these animals, and accepts only the best from her class. However, this is not always the case.

The children, too, will not all necessarily share the same level of compassion and commitment to their class pet. A classroom filled with kids who love animals and are on a quest to learn about their proper care makes an ideal situation for a classroom hamster. Indeed, an animal in such a class will typically fare well when allowed to go home with different children every weekend, which is often

Hamsters can be great pets for kids in the classroom, as long as the teacher arranges their care over weekends and holidays and all home trips are supervised by a parent.

> **Meet Hamtaro**
>
> Although images of hamsters in the media are not all that common, these animals do have one claim to media fame: They are the stars of the popular Japanese children's books and cartoon program *Hamtaro.*
>
> Within the world of Hamtaro, we find the ongoing story of a neighborhood population of golden hamsters who meet secretly to discuss their many adventures. The fun and popularity of Hamtaro has led to a rise in keeping hamsters as pets in Japan (that, and the fact that this is the perfect pet for a decidedly urban, densely populated country). It has also inspired a collection of action figures depicting the adorable Ham-Hams, as they are called, in a variety of vocations and activities, and even a book on hamster care for young children who find themselves enamored not only of Hamtaro, but also of the genuine article who inspired those adorable little club members.

the policy in classrooms that host class pets. This weekend visit can be thrilling for a child—not so thrilling for a hamster if the kid, or the kid's parents, don't know how to take care of the weekend visitor or how to ensure her security.

The best teacher will exercise unilateral veto power if a child proves to be a potential threat to a class hamster. Better yet, perhaps this teacher will decide that maybe a class hamster really isn't all that necessary this year.

Hamster-Friendly Times

The twenty-first century promises to be an especially friendly time for these tiny animals. As more and more people move to urban and suburban areas where larger pets may not be welcome, many still long to live with animals. The hamster is a natural in meeting that need.

Her small size, cleanliness, and ease of care mean that she can thrive in a tiny, metropolitan studio apartment with a "no pets" policy just as easily as she can in a large, suburban multi-bedroom home that hosts a variety of pets. And, according

Hamsters groom themselves, adding to their popularity.

to veteran hamster caretakers, she fills the pet bill quite nicely, proven by the fact that the hamster is repeatedly named a popular household pet because she provides her own warm brand of easy-care companionship.

Another reason hamsters enjoy ever-increasing popularity is the rise of the dwarf hamsters. When these tiny, rather social, decidedly adorable animals squeaked on to the American pet scene a few short years ago, word spread like wildfire. Once upon a time, locating a pair of these diminutive creatures was quite a challenge. Today, however, thanks to a meteoric rise in their popularity, the various species of dwarfs are readily available from breeders and large pet supply stores.

Few associations exist for the promotion and protection of these small creatures, and there are far fewer fictionalized hamster characters than there are, say, mice and rabbits, yet their numbers are solid. And growing. The quiet popularity of the hamster as an invited resident in human households indicates that, within American homes, there are thousands of well-loved hamsters living peacefully and quietly, converting one person, one family, at a time to the joy that is hamster keeping.

Chapter 3

Why Have a Hamster?

You've no doubt heard it, if not experienced it yourself—the voice of a child, begging, pleading, whining, pulling out all the stops. The harried parents standing there listening to the now-oh-so-familiar refrain: "I promise I'll take care of him. Really, Mom, I mean it. You won't have to do anything!"

It's the age-old plea for a hamster.

We come to know hamsters from our earliest memories, whether our families live with them or not. Their familiarity is universal. But think about it. Why is that? Just what is it about this animal that makes him such a unique, unforgettable pet?

With proper guidance, children (and their parents) can learn what surprisingly social and interactive pets these soft, warm little critters can be, and just why they command such a large population of admirers.

Why Do We Love Them?

The hamster's charm creeps up subtly. You admire this little animal's compact, barrel-like physique; his wide muzzle accentuated by a treat hidden within his cheeks; the tiny paws he so delicately uses to nibble on that treat; and his bright eyes and rather large nose. These characteristics compose a portrait of a pet who resembles a tiny stuffed toy or a miniature teddy bear who can actually live and breathe within your home.

After this first impression, you are likely to view the hamster as a quiet, benign, unobtrusive creature, and suddenly, you find yourself gripped by something so very lovable about this little rodent. As though sensing your thoughts, he stands up on his haunches and begins nibbling a raisin that he holds in his tiny "hands." That's it. You're a goner. Whether you happen to be 9 years old or 60, you simply must spend the rest of your life—or at least the next two years—basking in that charm.

There really is no point to try and figure out why our species loves hamsters as we do. We may still ask how such a tiny animal can so charm and captivate generations of children (and, be honest, their parents), only to find that the answers are right in front of us. Just spend some time with the little creatures and it will all become crystal clear.

Taking Stock of Pocket Pets

First, hamsters—most hamsters, that is—don't have much of a tail. This fact alone explains plenty. Indeed, the same people who cringe at the thought of keeping a mouse or a rat as a pet are just as likely to warm to the idea that a pet hamster might be a great idea.

This seems perplexing, given the similarities of these animals. Rodents all, mice, rats, and hamsters share chisel-like incisors that require constant gnawing for proper maintenance, they all thrive under similar living situations in captivity, and they are best maintained on the same basic diet. Mice, however, tend to be more timid than hamsters and rats, who enjoy regular forays out of their cages with their human handlers—an activity that can prove frightening, even fatally stressful, for most mice. Hamsters are less gregarious and, with all due respect, not quite as intelligent as rats.

The stubby little remnant of a tail makes a hamster look a lot less like a rat or a mouse—making him a more acceptable rodent pet for many humans.

Yet for some people, the issue isn't necessarily sociability or intelligence. Indeed, as we have seen, the major difference between mice and rats and their hamster friend is an unexpected attribute that has nothing to do with lifestyle or personality. Yet for some would-be rodent owners, this characteristic elevates the hamster instantly above the mouse and rat. That trait is the tail, or, more specifically, the hamster's lack of one.

For all practical purposes (and with the exception of the Chinese dwarf, who sports a bona fide tail), the pet hamster has no tail. Instead, he has a short, tapered stub that contributes to the compact, cylindrical shape of the hamster's physique. This stubby rear end, the product of an underground burrowing existence, has repeatedly helped kids convince moms and dads through the years to grant permission for countless rodent pets. One look at that little creature sans tail, next to the rats and mice in the pet shop, and parents find themselves saying yes to the hamster.

A Face You've Got to Love

Once new owners get past the tail issue, they discover a small pet with a gentle, sweet temperament (if properly handled and socialized, as explained in chapter 6), coupled with an appearance that sets him apart as a unique individual among rodent companions.

This individuality is most vividly reflected in the hamster's face and head. His senses of smell and hearing have been largely responsible for the hamster's survival in his native territory. His eyes are large and expressive, complementing his button nose and perky, rounded ears that are perched erect, yet slightly askew, at the top of the head.

This combination lends the hamster a distinct expression of whimsy and fun. He's cute, pure and simple.

A Perfect Fit

Through the years, we humans have tended to make a transition from a rural existence to one that is more urban and suburban. Yet we still feel the need to live with animals, and indeed, research has repeatedly shown that we should live with animals. They are good for our heart, our blood pressure, our peace of mind, and our overall health and well-being.

But it has also become more and more difficult to find housing in these more urban areas that are willing to take us as well as our pets. Enter the hamster, the perfect pet for small spaces, as well as for domiciles where larger pets (or even smaller ones) are not allowed. Hamsters are clean, quiet, and take up very little room, yet they provide us with the connection to the animal world that we so desperately need. Just another reason why hamsters continue to be such popular pets.

Hamster Grooming Habits

Watch your hamster regularly and you will soon realize that this little animal grooms himself constantly. Before eating, after eating, before a nap, after a nap, before a spin in the hamster ball, after a spin in the hamster ball—the hamster

TIP

Remember that although you might believe a single golden hamster is lonely, he actually prefers living alone, so resist the temptation to place a new "friend" in his enclosure. This critter only needs and wants you as his friend, and once you have tamed him and earned his trust, the bond will be permanent.

stops, straightens any displaced hairs, and washes his face for the seventeenth time that day. This is a meticulously clean little guy. In fact, he's so diligent about cleanliness, both his own and his habitat's, that he could be dubbed the Felix Unger of the rodent world. Again, another reason why so many people find themselves attracted to these adorable critters.

Golden or Dwarf?

Once you say yes to hamster ownership, your decisions do not end there. You still need to determine whether you would like a single Syrian, or golden, hamster, or perhaps a pair of the ever-popular, oh-so-adorable dwarfs.

If you're looking for a pet who is somewhat more interactive with and focused on you, who is found in a variety of coat types and colors, and who can fit comfortably in your hand without leaving you worried that you will blink and he'll be gone, then the traditional golden hamster is for you.

If a dwarf hamster is the pet of your dreams, remember this: You can tame dwarfs, but you must continue the taming exercises throughout their lives, or the effects are not necessarily permanent. The darling dwarfs, you see, are actually more interested in those of their own kind, having evolved in the wild in colonies where they learned to enjoy and need each other. This preference has not changed among dwarfs kept in captivity, so respect them for that and find a pair (preferably two males or two females to prevent a hamster population explosion in your home) who are happily bonded. You will then likely find that your tiny friends are more active than their golden cousins.

The good news is that no matter which type of hamster you choose, the popularity of each ensures that you will probably be able to find just what you are looking for. You'll also be able to find the proper equipment and even toys.

Wanted: Responsible Owners

So you've decided the hamster is the right pet for you. But are you the right owner for a hamster? The quintessential happy, healthy hamster is one who resides with the quintessential responsible owner. This is a person who takes the time—before bringing a new pet home—to learn about the housing, diet, exercise, and social interaction the pet will require if he is to live a long and healthy life. Whether you are keeping a dog or a tiny dwarf hamster as a pet, every animal deserves optimum living conditions, regular attention, and veterinary care.

As this responsible owner, you should learn the basics of hamster care and be willing to do it right. Take seriously the hamster's need for cleanliness and commit to keeping his habitat sanitary every day. Change the bedding in his home regularly, offer him good, fresh food and water every day, and remove uneaten food every day, too. Do your pet a favor by respecting his nocturnal habits. This means reserving playtimes for the late afternoon and evening, when your small pet is most amenable to activity.

A responsible owner can be an adult or a child (many a child has actually proven to be the superior caretaker). A hamster is a fine pet for children, but the animal's care must never be relegated exclusively to a child, no matter how responsible that child might be. While caring for a hamster presents a child with the ideal opportunity to learn the importance of providing a pet with food, water, attention, and a clean environment, this must *always* be done with adult supervision. You cannot teach a child a lesson about responsibility at the expense of the hamster. He is a living being, and deserves the best possible care, no matter what.

The greatest part of being a responsible owner is the commitment made to the hamster. You must remain dedicated to providing your pet with all the necessary amenities, avoiding unintentional breeding, and spending time every day with your pet. In return, you will learn firsthand how attached people can become to these wee creatures, and what a delightful relationship can exist between what was once a solitary desert dweller and the lucky person who takes him in. This often comes as a surprise to first-time owners, who find themselves hooked for life after that first experience of living in harmony with a hamster.

Caring for a hamster is a great way to learn to be responsible for a living being. But an adult must always supervise, for the well-being of the hamster.

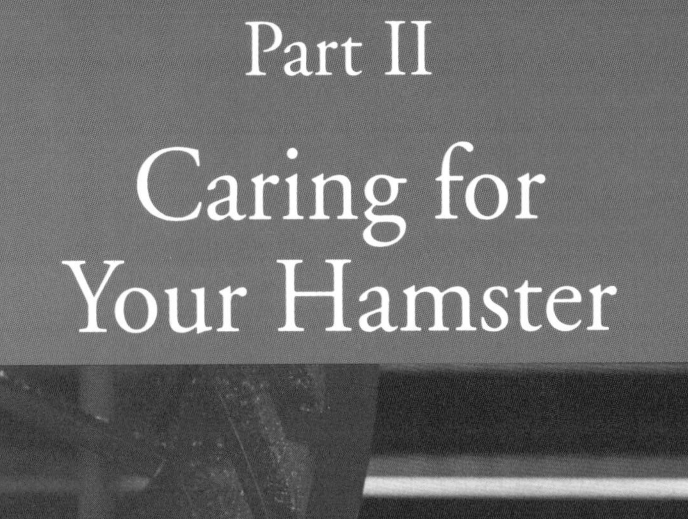

Part II

Caring for Your Hamster

Chapter 4

Your Hamster's Home

Hamsters are determined homebodies, content only if living within the ultimate hamster domicile: everything in its place, all corners squeaky clean. Yet the hamster, even the happy hamster, is the consummate escape artist. Escape is seen as a grand game, reminiscent of what sent your pet's ancestors over miles and miles of desert terrain in search of food and adventure in the wild. The challenge is to place your hamster in an enclosure without even the tiniest possible escape route, and to maintain those digs in a way that keeps the premises pristine as well as inviting.

You'll need to set up your hamster's habitat *before* you bring her home, so all will be ready for her arrival.

Hamster Habitats

Your goal is to provide the hamster with a home that is not only impenetrable, but also so attractive, well furnished, and clean that your pet won't ever entertain even the possibility of escape. In other words, make your hamster's home her castle and all else will fall into place.

When planning her habitat, keep these two words in mind: *neat* and *clean.* Your hamster will rest only when everything within her environment is arranged with distinct spots for eating, drinking, and sleeping; another section for playing; and yet another designated as a bathroom. The basic rule in hamster housing, then, is that bigger is better.

There are various types of housing for these animals, and opinions vary on which is best. But regardless of housing style, veteran hamster keepers agree that you should strive to provide the hamster with as much room as possible—a minimum of 19 square inches on the floor of her habitat. A roomy enclosure also offers you the opportunity to design the interior with all the separate areas your pet will require.

Glass or Acrylic Tank

A popular setup for hamster keeping—and one in which you will most often find these small pets displayed—is the glass aquarium or terrarium. (A variation on this is an acrylic tank that comes fully equipped with a ventilated handle top and other internal accessories.) For a single golden hamster or a pair of dwarfs, the aquarium tank should be at least the 10-gallon size. It must be well constructed (no sharp edges at the corners, no cracked sides), and it must have a well-fitting top, possibly made of screen but preferably wire (the wire is sturdier), with no gaps or holes that can inspire escape. The best top for an aquarium setup is framed with metal that slides on and off. This type ensures not only security—skilled as she may be, the hamster cannot slide off the properly installed top—but also provides ventilation, which is critical to hamster health.

Indeed a potential lack of ventilation can be a drawback of the aquarium setup. In addition, while the aquarium walls may help prevent odor from wafting

Don't Do It Yourself

Veteran hamster keepers recommend that you steer clear of homemade hamster habitats. Unless you are an expert on rodent behavior and physiology and on how these animals interact with various materials they might find in their environment, you are wise to rely on the judgment of those who are, and choose a commercially made product that will prove to be safer and more secure for the hamster.

Commercial enclosures of gnaw-proof glass, metal, or wire are superior to a homemade wooden structure that may be treated with chemicals—and less expensive in the long run. Stick with the more traditional setups, and avoid any unexpected, not to mention easily prevented, tragedies.

out into the household, you must be willing to follow a strict pickup routine and clean the tank regularly and thoroughly to vanquish the potentially hidden odors within the aquarium walls and protect your hamster's health.

The great benefits of aquarium-style housing include the fact that these enclosures are easy to clean; they keep those odors at bay; and they retain hay, bedding, food, and residual dust within the hamster's house, thus preventing these materials from overwhelming yours. Furthermore, if the enclosure is properly covered, this style of hamster home keeps the hamster safe and confined, yet quite visible to the many admirers who will want to come and observe the little critter as she plays, eats, and naps.

Traditional Wire Cage

While countless hamster keepers swear by the aquarium-style hamster house, there are just as many who would choose nothing other than a traditional wire cage (see page 42 for information on why this housing style may not work for dwarf hamsters). Ventilation, they say, is the number one reason for choosing the cage. And indeed, a roomy, airy enclosure helps prevent respiratory illness in hamsters.

A wire cage is well ventilated, which is important for hamster health.

As with any choice of hamster domicile, the cage must be well made and have no exposed wires or tears that could lead to injury and/or escape. The floor should be solid to hold in bedding and to facilitate burrowing, and the door should be one that can be latched securely. Even though this design is obviously light and airy, however, this does not mean you may forego routine cleaning. *Any style of housing must be cleaned regularly* (more on how to go about that in chapter 6).

A variation of the cage setup is the double-decker cage. Its proponents claim that it adds the advantage of extra space. Critics, however, warn that such a configuration can be dangerous to a hamster, a species not renowned for her climbing abilities. While such a setup is considered ideal for the hamster's larger cousin, the chinchilla, the critics claim, it can prove dangerous for the smaller hamster, who is a burrower, not a climber. She could take a serious tumble from the higher regions of such a cage. It may be wisest, then, to stick with the traditional single-story design and make life safer for your pet.

Tube Setups

When you think of hamsters, you may also tend to think of the modular tube setup—a configuration of plastic tubes, compartments, and similar segments that you assemble in various arrangements. This lets your hamster climb through a maze that is not all that different from the vast burrows and tunnels hamsters inhabit in the wild.

This setup is obviously fun for a hamster because it satisfies her natural instincts to burrow and travel through narrow tunnels, but it also has its drawbacks. Lack of ventilation can be a real problem, and resident hamsters can more easily evade capture when it's time to remove them from their home. Cleaning, too, can be a challenge, because the unit must be taken apart for thorough cleaning—and reassembled once cleaning is done. Failure to clean it properly results in an overpowering smell from urine and bits of food left in the various tubes of the habitat.

Tube setups are fun for a hamster, but may be tough to keep clean and properly ventilated. Certainly, though, they make a good part-time play gym.

Owners of dwarf hamsters often sing the praises of a tube setup because it is ostensibly escape-proof and perfect for hamsters who need constructive outlets for their high energy levels. Yet hamsters have been known to chew through the plastic of these systems, which can obviously lead to escape and/or digestive upset.

You may opt for a compromise, in which the tube setup is not the hamster's primary residence, but rather serves as more of a part-time playground. The hamster can eat and sleep in her more traditional cage or tank, and enjoy play-time in the tube habitat. Such a combination provides the hamster—and you—with the best of both worlds.

The Special Needs of Dwarf Hamsters

Unlike their fiercely solitary golden cousins, dwarf hamsters are best housed together in pairs. Once you have a bonded pair, whether they were born and raised that way or enticed into coexistence, they should not be separated (and indeed, once bonded, they find it very difficult adjusting to new partners). Dwarfs also tend to require more space than goldens, both because they are housed in pairs and because of their more playful, active natures.

Needless to say, housing this pair comfortably should be foremost in your mind, with security as your primary concern. Consider the tiny size of these animals. That small size translates to great artistry should one decide to escape her domicile. An aquarium or acrylic tank with a well-fitting screen or wire lid is considered the safest choice, because it is risky to assume that the bars of a cage are close enough together to keep these tiny, very flexible critters confined. So play it safe and keep them safe. You never want to have to look back and say, "If only . . . "

Where to Place Your Hamster's Habitat

The basic structure of your hamster's habitat is critical, but so is its placement. First, it goes without saying that the hamster must live indoors. Yes, wild hamsters live outside, but they spend a great deal of time underground. The domestic hamster simply does not do well exposed to the elements, especially when those elements involve extreme temperatures, rain and snow, and predators. A layer of bedding alone will not keep your hamster safe, so keep your pet indoors in a properly appointed, properly positioned habitat, where she will be safe and happy.

Hamster Nightlife

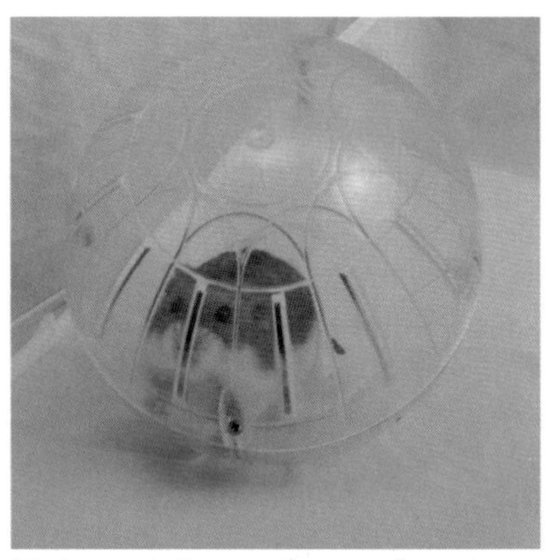

The hamster ball is a popular option for evening playtime. Hamsters still need to be supervised, even in the ball.

Keep in mind the basically nocturnal nature of the hamster when you decide where to place your pet's habitat. The hamster who is allowed to follow her own natural rhythms will sleep during the day and play in the early evening and at night. Therefore, place her enclosure in a section of the house that is quiet, dimly lit, and protected from the traffic and noise of the family's daytime activities. Your tiny pet should not have to tolerate the wild chases and hollering that may take place in high-traffic areas of your household.

When the hamster awakens full of energy and ready to play in the afternoon or early evening, make sure she has toys and food to keep her stimulated and satisfied. This is also the perfect opportunity for you to take the hamster out of her enclosure for some safe and properly supervised interactions with her family, or for a romp in her tube habitat.

As the evening progresses, you must also think of your own sleep patterns. You can remedy the squeaking wheel situation—and ensure you get a good night's sleep—by placing the hamster's cage far enough away from your own sleeping area and providing the animal with a variety of toys so she doesn't become addicted to the wheel. Of course, you can also try offering the wheel to your pet only when you are awake.

Temperature Requirements

Your hamster's enclosure should remain safely out of direct sunlight at all times. Heat and exposure to direct sun can be extremely harmful to your pet's health. When considering the right spot, keep in mind that the sunlight will move during the day, so a shaded spot by a window in the morning could be flooded with sun in the afternoon.

Avoid drafts, as well, either from open windows or air-conditioning vents. Drafts are particularly dangerous to hamsters, as they can contribute to potentially life-threatening respiratory problems. The ideal draft-free temperature for hamsters is anywhere from 65 to 80 degrees Fahrenheit (for newborn hamsters, the ideal temperature is 70 to 75 degrees). Although they are underground

How to Set Up Your Hamster's Home

One of your long-term goals as a hamster owner is to keep your tiny pet's stress to a minimum. The first step you can take is to prepare your new pet's habitat before you even think of bringing her home. Plan ahead, prepare, and you will provide your new companion with the ultimate welcome. Just follow these simple steps.

1. Do your research and decide which style of hamster housing you think will be best for your situation, your home, and your hamster (or hamsters, if you intend to bring home a pair of dwarfs). Evaluate your choices in terms of maintenance, spaciousness (minimum 19 inches of floor space), and design.
2. Go to the pet supply store and buy your hamster's new home (a cage or a terrarium/aquarium-style enclosure).
3. Buy all the necessary furnishings and supplies for your hamster's home: bedding (hamster-safe bedding, of course; no cedar or pine products), toys, hiding places (boxes, PVC tubes, cardboard oatmeal canisters, and the like), food and water receptacles, and so on.

desert dwellers in the wild, hamsters thrive best in the same basic room temperatures preferred by the humans in their lives.

Hamster-Proofing

When determining where to place your hamster's home, make sure that no particularly dangerous household items are within reach of the animal's cage, and thus within reach of the hamster. You certainly don't want electrical cords hanging into or near the enclosure that could be oh-so-inviting to the hamster's gnawing impulses. Nor do you want your pet's home to be situated near cleaning solvents or similar chemical agents with fumes that could prove damaging to the hamster's sensitive respiratory tract.

4. Choose the ideal location for your hamster's home. This must be a spot that is out of direct sunlight and drafts; away from the noisy, high-traffic areas of the house; and with an air temperature of 65 to 80 degrees Fahrenheit.
5. Clean the habitat structure and all the permanent furnishings with a mild detergent. Rinse and dry the items thoroughly.
6. Place the habitat in the chosen spot.
7. Carpet the floor of your pet's enclosure with a three-inch layer of clean, safe bedding material.
8. Check the security. Make sure the door of the cage can be fastened securely or that the screen or wire roof of the terrarium/aquarium can be safely secured to prevent escape.
9. Put on your interior decorator hat. With your new pet's fastidious nature in mind, place her bed in one corner of the enclosure, the food dishes in another corner, and her toys in yet another corner. Leave one area free as the designated bathroom. If you will be offering water with a water bottle, hang the bottle on the enclosure wall. Upon entering her new home, your hamster, the recipient of your thoughtful hamster housewarming, will have no choice but to feel right at home.
10. Once your hamster comes home, allow her a few days of peace and quiet to adjust to the scents and sights of her new surroundings. Then enjoy your new pet.

She should also be safely situated out of the reach of other household pets—particularly cats, dogs, and snakes; they may not be able to reach your hamster to harm her physically, but their mere presence outside of the enclosure is enough to cause stress and serious health problems.

Put simply, make sure the enclosure is in a safe place. Period.

Additional Supplies

There is far more to the ideal hamster habitat than walls alone. The furnishings within those walls are just as vital to keeping your hamster healthy and mentally stimulated. Before you bring your hamster home, make sure you have all the necessary supplies on hand: food and water receptacles, nesting/bedding material, an exercise wheel, perhaps a hamster ball, toys, and a supply of fresh food.

Water Bottle

Hamsters need to have fresh water available at all times, and a water bottle that attaches to the wall of the enclosure is a simple way to supply this. Pet supply stores sell various sizes of water bottles, and medium is considered ideal for a traditional hamster's cage (perhaps something smaller for a pair of dwarfs; you be the judge).

If you prefer to offer your hamster his water in a dish, remember that some hamsters end up viewing this as an indoor spa, sitting in the water and splashing around. Not very sanitary. If you still prefer the dish, use one that is weighted on the bottom to prevent tipping, and commit to checking and changing the water frequently throughout the day. You might also consider a dish designed for birds that fastens to the side of the cage, but make sure it is positioned low enough for the hamster to reach. Better yet, why not just use a water bottle?

Food Dishes

Hamsters tend to enjoy sitting in their food dishes as well as eating from them. Chalk this up to caching behavior, or perhaps simply the desire to guard food from other hamsters who might wish to take a bite. If your hamster is one of these, your best bet is to buy a good, solid dish that is well weighted at the base to prevent tipping and easy to clean. Nontoxic ceramic dishes are usually ideal.

The hamster food dish should be big enough to hold plenty of food and sturdy enough to avoid tipping.

The bowl you choose for your hamster should be large enough not necessarily to hold the hamster herself, but certainly to hold an ample supply of food for your pet's daily energy needs. Make sure the dish is shallow enough as well, so that your hamster can reach the food at the bottom and receive her full daily rations. For advice on what to put in the bowl, see chapter 7.

Bedding

The choice and type of bedding you choose for your hamster is crucial to her health and well-being. This is, after all, a burrowing animal who takes great pleasure in digging into a mound of bedding for a nap, for a game of hide-and-seek, or for hiding a cache of food. Your choice of bedding is not only directly connected to the hamster's pleasure in these activities, but also to her overall health.

While hamsters are burrowing animals, this does not mean you need to recreate her natural environment in your home. Avoid the temptation to carpet the floor of the hamster's enclosure with a thick layer of natural materials, such as dirt or sand, through which she can burrow and build her own maze of tunnels. These materials can actually prove to be *too* natural, containing parasites, bacteria, and other disease-carrying agents that could prove deadly to the resident hamster.

Bedding should be clean, dry, nontoxic, and absorbent. The most popular bedding choice, and one that typically satisfies these criteria, is wood shavings.

If wood is your preference, opt for aspen shavings that are produced specifically for the care of small animals. Don't carpet the enclosure with remnants from a lumberyard or a woodworking shop. The hamster can suffer severe repercussions from the dust and chemicals in these types of wood products. Similar problems can arise from cat litter, another inappropriate bedding choice for hamsters.

Other safer, and possibly more pleasant, bedding options include products made from vegetable materials or shredded paper. If you choose the paper option, pick products made from plain, unprinted newspaper stock (avoid using your own newspaper or scratch paper, as ink can be toxic to hamsters). Commercial bedding products, which are readily available at pet supply stores, are typically available in pelleted form, designed and formulated for hygiene, absorption, dust reduction, and odor control. You may supplement the bedding with a few handfuls of hay, but, like

CAUTION

Do not use cedar shavings for bedding, as this aromatic wood can prove too intense for small rodents. Pine, too, is typically considered a less-than-perfect choice, especially in this enlightened age when so many safer alternatives are available.

everything you place in your hamster's habitat, the hay, too, must be clean, dry, and free of parasites and mold. Place the hay in one section of the enclosure to designate the nesting area.

Regardless of the type of bedding material you choose, cover the floor of the hamster's habitat with three inches or so of clean, fresh bedding. This will provide your pet with ample room in which to burrow, play, and hide. A generous, clean layer of bedding also provides a sound foundation for all the other furnishings you will be placing in your hamster's abode.

Hideaways (Nest Boxes)

As a nocturnal creature with an affinity for burrowing, the hamster must have somewhere to hide when she feels the need to escape from the prying eyes of her admirers. In addition to the carpet of bedding in her abode, provide your pet with a variety of beds in which she can build a cozy nest.

The choice of these items must be made with hamster physiology in mind. Remember those teeth of hers and their ability to shred. Keep away from materials that could fall victim to chewing. Soft plastic and cardboard, for example, won't last long with a hamster about. Hard plastic, PVC piping, and the various items made specifically for hamster habitats are superior choices—and less expensive in the long run because they don't need to be constantly replaced.

Every hamster needs a hideaway.

The nest/hiding boxes themselves come in many styles. You may want to provide your hamster with two choices for variety. For example, your hamster may enjoy one box with solid walls in which she can completely hide from the outside world, and another with clear, hard plastic walls and several openings that she can use as a makeshift playhouse.

Position the nest boxes in the hamster's home—preferably some distance away from the food dishes and the water bottle, as these should occupy their own special spots within the habitat. Keep them away from the presumed playing area and the area you deem to be the hamster's chosen bathroom, and you will help foster your pet's desire for order and cleanliness.

The best nest hideaways are those that provide the hamster with an accessible opening and plenty of privacy once she is inside. Some of these are available commercially, in sizes appropriate for goldens and in smaller models for dwarf hamsters. Start shopping and you'll find a variety of styles, designs, and shapes to satisfy even the most finicky hamster. As an added benefit, high-quality commercial styles are made of safe, nontoxic materials that can withstand long-term rodent gnawing.

You might also find items around your home that can be used as hamster hideaways—although the safe examples of these are usually temporary as they get gnawed into nothingness. An empty tissue box, an empty toilet-paper roll, or a cylindrical oatmeal container, for example, can provide the hamster with a fun change of pace, but, for obvious reasons, they probably won't last long. Use your imagination when choosing household items for your pet, but always keep the basic rules of hamster safety and destructive abilities in mind.

Toys to Make a Hamster Happy

Hamsters are active creatures, who, despite their easy-care reputation, thrive on stimulation. They enjoy interactions with their owners (once they have come to trust them) and new and exciting items within their environment. Offer your pet a variety of toys to hold her interest and keep her active. As you can probably guess by now, these toys, like everything in the hamster's environment, must be properly constructed and made of nontoxic materials.

> **CAUTION**
>
> Dwarf hamsters require far smaller toys and wheels than do their larger golden cousins. If you offer your dwarf hamsters the larger models of some items (especially the wheel), you can end up with injured hamsters.

The classic hamster toy is, of course, the exercise wheel. Wheels are available in various sizes. The smallest are designed for dwarf

Hamsters absolutely must have safe materials to gnaw on, so they can keep their teeth healthy.

hamsters, who can be severely injured on larger models. Running on the wheel, however, can be addictive to a hamster, not to mention noisy for you when the hamster runs all night. For the sanity of all involved, make wheel time a treat for your pet, placing the wheel in the cage only every now and then. Check the wheel carefully before offering it to the hamster, as damage and sharp edges can lead to a damaged hamster. So by all means give your hamster a wheel to run, but offer her other toys as well.

Another toy that has become popular is the so-called hamster ball. This is a hollow, clear plastic ball into which a hamster may securely sit and "run" through the house safely. Problems arise when a hamster is left in the ball without supervision, which can lead to injury and/or escape. Even when safely ensconced in her hamster ball, your pet must be monitored at all times when she is out of her habitat.

Other favorite toys include commercially available ladders, bridges, and novelty hideaways that may be used for hiding and climbing. Some trusty household items—such as PVC piping and cardboard toilet-paper and paper-towel rolls—are also great for play, providing perfect props for rousing games of hide-and-seek.

As educated hamster owners are well aware, rodents must gnaw to keep their teeth trimmed, and some toys do dual duty in this area. Fruit tree branches and chunks of wood can satisfy a hamster's chewing impulses, and at the same time

Seeking Safe Play

Safety should always be first on your mind when choosing hamster toys. Make sure the toys are the right size for your hamster: smaller hamster balls and wheels for dwarfs and larger items for their bigger golden cousins. Check the wheel regularly to ensure it remains in good working order, with no exposed wires or sharp edges that could hurt the toes or tummy of a particularly athletic hamster, or catch the long hair of a teddy bear.

Periodically place new toys within your hamster's abode, replacing familiar items with new exciting ones and rotating the toys every day or two to retain your pet's interest. Make sure, however, that the toys sit securely in the flooring material so they do not roll over or fall onto a hamster if she uses it in a way that was not intended.

make attractive additions to the hamster habitat. These items provide the hamster with new and different surfaces on which to climb as well as gnaw, but, for the hamster's protection, the wood or branch must be clean, untreated, and nontoxic. You may find that such safe pieces are even available for purchase at well-stocked pet supply stores. Look for natural bird perches, because they make good hamster toys as well, and remember that your hamster *must* have something to gnaw on for her health.

Make sure all toys you buy for your hamster are the right size for your golden or dwarf. This little tube is fine for Zippy, a dwarf, but would be too narrow for a golden hamster.

Chapter 5

Choosing Your Hamster

You have decided that the hamster is the perfect pet for you and your family. You've bought everything you need and set up your hamster's habitat. All that's missing now is the hamster.

Making Preparations

Before bringing your new hamster home, some preparations are in order. Buying a hamster on impulse because you spot a darling little cream-colored teddy bear who wiggles his whiskers at you as you pass by a pet shop window is not the wise way to go. Before you take the plunge, think about the commitment you will be making, even to what is a relatively inexpensive pet.

The first step, once you have decided to share your life for the next two or three years or so with a hamster, is to take stock of what you will need to provide a safe and secure home for your new pet. You will need to assemble his habitat (see chapter 4) and stock up on food (see chapter 7) and supplies.

Leaving the environment to which he has become accustomed can be a dangerously stressful experience for a hamster. Ease your hamster's anxiety by taking care of the details long before you bring your new pet home.

If the hamster is destined for a home with children, which is the norm for this animal, by all means involve the kids in the preparation process. Remember, though, that a hamster must never be relegated solely to the care of a child. While these easy-care pets provide kids with a fine opportunity to learn and experience the responsibility of caring for a helpless creature, even the most

What You Need Before Your Hamster Comes Home

- Your hamster's house
- Food and water, plus appropriate food and water receptacles
- Safe toys and exercise equipment
- Safe and appropriate bedding material
- The name of a reliable veterinarian who is qualified in hamster care

dependable kids have been known to fall down on the job from time to time. Parents must remain involved to ensure that the hamster continues to receive the optimum care he requires and deserves.

Finally, enjoy the anticipation. Working together as a family, purchasing the equipment, preparing a new pet's home, learning the ins and outs of proper care—there are few joys more thrilling for kids and adults alike. Take it slowly, proceed with common sense, and you are sure to make the arrival of your new pet a truly memorable experience for the entire family.

Like all pets, hamsters deserve good veterinary care. Before you bring your hamster home, find a local vet who is familiar with pocket pets.

Quality Veterinary Services

Before you bring your new pet home, you should also take the time to find a veterinarian. Ask other hamster owners for references, then visit several clinics to get a feel for each practice. You need to find a veterinarian who has the proper experience, equipment, medications, and staff with expertise in pocket-pet care. This expertise includes a working knowledge of diseases hamsters may contract and how they respond to medications, as well as dietary needs, behavior, and reproduction. After-hours emergency service is another plus. Once you locate this veterinary practice, you may even want to stop by with your new pet right away for a baseline evaluation of the hamster's health.

Where to Get Your New Pet

Once you have decided whether you want a golden hamster with long or short hair, or perhaps a pair of dwarf Russians, you should begin the search for your companion. You have several options.

Pet Store

The most popular place to get a hamster is the pet store. While many pet shops these days do not to sell puppies and kittens, most still carry small pocket pets.

The benefit of the pet shop is convenience. Find a good shop with a knowledgeable staff, and you can take advantage of one-stop shopping. You can buy all

A breeder is more likely to have the less common types of hamsters, such as Hammy, who is a teddy bear.

the supplies necessary for your hamster's care, and then go back to the same place to get your little guy.

Look for a shop with a staff who can answer questions about the care of the pets they are selling. They should offer sound advice on hamster care and be able to tell the difference between male hamsters and female hamsters. The shop should be sanitary—evident in the animals' clean food, water, and bedding, and general lack of odor. The pets in the shop should look healthy and well adjusted, their habitats clean and uncrowded.

Golden hamsters in the pet shop should, in most cases, be housed separately. Separate housing indicates that the staff understands the solitary nature of these hamsters, and it also reduces the risk that you'll discover an unexpected hamster pregnancy when you get your new pet home. The exception may be younger golden siblings, who can be housed together. You are likely to find the more sociable dwarf hamsters housed together (preferably in pairs), as well. This will indicate that the hamsters are probably safely bonded and may go to a new home together.

Breeder

If you are looking for a more exotic hamster—say, a teddy bear (longhaired) hamster of a specific color or pattern—then a breeder may be your best bet. Hamster breeders may be difficult to locate, so you might have to do some hunting.

In your search for a hamster breeder, check your local newspaper and the Internet. You may also want to ask at pet shops that carry hamsters, because the breeders from whom they obtain their animals may breed more exotic varieties as well. Ask local veterinarians, too, especially those who treat hamsters. They should know breeders in the area who are their clients (this also shows that the breeder is willing to seek veterinary care for their animals—a good sign).

Another locale for finding breeders—especially several breeders all together—is at a county or state fair. Pet shows, where a variety of hamsters are brought together at one big event, are another option. The individuals handling the hamsters at these shows and fairs are usually their breeders, most of whom couldn't be happier to speak with prospective buyers who appreciate the quality of healthy, well-bred show hamsters.

Animal Shelter

As part of the sad and endless cycle of too many hamsters and not enough homes, abandoned or homeless hamsters may find themselves at the doorsteps of local animal shelters. What happens to them at that point depends on the shelter and the resources available to it.

Some shelters run hamster adoption programs and encourage would-be hamster owners to visit the animals they offer for adoption. But others, because they are overwhelmed with the vast numbers of dogs and cats who come their way, have no choice but to humanely kill small rodents. They simply do not have the staff, money, or space to accommodate hamsters. Contact your local shelters as possible sources for a hamster—and consider the hamster overpopulation problem if you are thinking of breeding your pet.

Choosing a Healthy Hamster

Regardless of where you get your hamster, choose carefully. Whether your hamster comes from a pet store, a breeder, a county fair, or an animal shelter, consider the following points when evaluating potential pets.

Age

No matter how you slice it, hamsters do not have long life spans. Most live only two to three years. It's no wonder, then, that most people prefer to choose a younger hamster as a pet. In addition to the life span issue, the young pet's minimal experience with humans makes it easier for you to socialize him. This does not mean an older hamster is out of the question, though. With gentle handling, an older hamster can bond to new people as well, especially if his experience with humans has been positive.

As for the older hamster whose experiences with humans have not been so positive, you can enjoy a mutually satisfying relationship with this animal as well, but only on his terms. He may never enjoy the handling in which some hamsters delight, yet he can still partake in daily forays out of his enclosure and take comfort in the fact that he is cared for each day by an owner who does not force him into uncomfortable situations. You, in turn, may take pride in knowing that you are rekindling a hamster's faith in humans.

Male or Female?

While hamsters exhibit differences in behaviors during mating, most veteran hamster owners do not see a dramatic difference between the two as pets. This is probably because, in the case of goldens anyway, they are solitary animals who are typically and ideally housed individually.

Recognizing male from female can be tricky, especially in very young hamsters. In the female, the distance between the anus and the sexual opening is much smaller than it is in the male. You can also see that the male has a more pointed rear end. After the fourth or fifth week (when the male hamster is sexually mature) the male's testicles are clearly visible on either side of the anus.

While you may not have a preference, gender can obviously play an important role in avoiding unexpected pregnancies. If you house two goldens together, you run the risk not only of ending up with an injured pet, but also with an unplanned litter of hamsters. As for a pair of dwarfs, make sure you have expert advice on whether they are sisters, brothers, or a male/female couple.

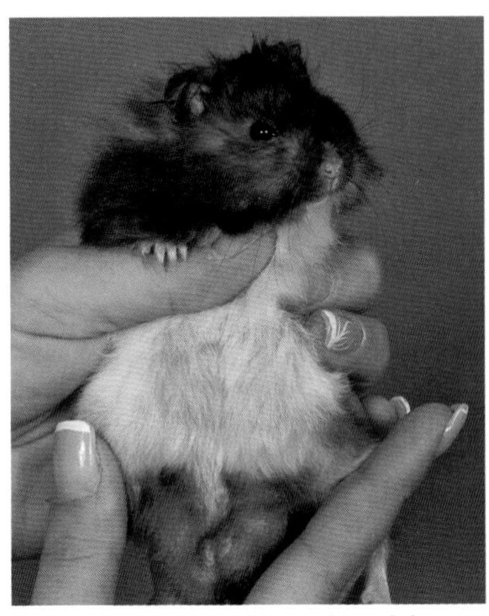

You can clearly see the testicles on this male hamster.

You are best off working with breeders, pet shop staff, and shelter personnel who are well versed in telling males from females—especially with dwarfs, who should be housed together. If you are in doubt, follow the separate housing rule.

Physical Condition

Health is of the utmost importance when choosing a hamster. A hamster who is healthy when you first bring him into your home is more likely to remain that way. When evaluating potential pets, look for the hamster with sparkling, lively eyes; clean ears held erect and alert; even, well-formed, well-trimmed incisors (the sign of a proper bite and healthy gnawing habits); and a proportioned, compact, barrel-shaped body.

Stress, diet, and general care are also indicated by the condition of the hamster's coat. A healthy hamster's coat should be evenly furred and clean (from his frequent self-grooming sessions), with no evidence of hair loss (some hair loss can be normal in an aging hamster). Even though the animal may not be inclined to climb right into your hand in the spirit of "love at first sight," he should demonstrate a fun-loving curiosity about his environment, especially about toys.

If you visit the hamster at noon and he seems rather listless and tired, don't simply assume the little animal is lazy or unhealthy and thus not the pet for you. Remember that this is a nocturnal creature who would rather be sleeping than impressing would-be owners at this time of day. Come back later in the afternoon or evening to witness his true character.

Signs of a Healthy Hamster

	Healthy Hamster	Unhealthy Hamster
Eyes	Lively and shiny	Sticky discharge, puffy
Nose	Dry	Wet
Rear end	Dry	Damp
Fur	Abundant, silky or fluffy	Dull and course
Body	Cylindrical, filled out	Thin
Behavior	Vigorous, curious, hearty appetite	Lethargic, unresponsive, no appetite

What you must avoid is a hamster with a wet rear end, as this is not likely caused by the hamster's habit of sitting in his water dish. The animal may be afflicted by the severe bacterial ailment called wet tail. If caught early, this can be treated with antibiotics and fluid therapy, but knowingly choosing a pet with the condition, and perhaps exposing other hamsters you already own, can spell trouble, because wet tail is highly contagious and potentially fatal to hamsters. Avoid any other hamsters from the same enclosure, as they, too, may be affected.

Evaluate the hamster's environment, as well. Stress can take a heavy toll on a hamster's health. You may not notice any outward signs of health problems in the hamster from a crowded, unclean enclosure, but a pet coming from such an environment will probably not live as long as one from a clean, stress-free habitat.

Welcoming Your New Pet Home

Common sense should prevail on that grand day when you are ready to pick up your pet and bring him home. The habitat is clean and organized and in a proper corner of the house; fresh food and water await; a layer of clean bedding sits ready to invite the attentions of a burrowing little creature; and the toys are ready for play. This is the ideal day to begin earning your new hamster's respect. Work toward this ultimate goal from your first meeting, and you just might be rewarded with a bond between pet and owner that you find both surprising and rewarding.

When you pick up your hamster, bring a small ventilated container with you to transport your new pet. Most stores will have so-called travel cages available, but again, you want to be prepared. If the trip will be a short one, a heavy cardboard box with holes for ventilation will suffice. But to prevent the hamster from attempting an escape by chewing, a heavier, plastic, well-ventilated container may be a better choice. This will also come in handy down the road as a holding pen for the hamster when you are cleaning his cage.

Place some bedding material in this small travel box—if possible some bedding from the hamster's enclosure at the pet shop, shelter, or breeding facility. This will provide not only a comfortable ride, but a familiar scent as well. Stash a couple of treats in your pocket, too, perhaps a peanut in the shell or a sunflower seed to keep your new pet occupied for the journey home.

After visiting the veterinarian (if the preliminary exam is part of your plan), take the hamster directly to his new home. Don't stop off at a party first or visit a child's classroom to show off the new pet. Keep in mind the animal's well-being and the alleviation of his stress. Your job is to get your hamster home as soon as possible, place him in his new enclosure, and then leave him alone for a while to get accustomed to his surroundings.

Assuming you have already wisely placed the hamster's habitat in a quiet, untraveled corner of the house, the hamster will probably explore his new enclosure a bit, check out his food, and perhaps burrow into some shavings for a little nap. Providing the hamster with the opportunity to partake of these simple introductions is your first step toward earning your new pet's lifelong respect.

Take your time in interacting with your new hamster. Even if he seems ready for play, introduce yourself gradually. You will both benefit in the long run. It may be disappointing just to leave your new hamster alone for a while, but it won't be forever. In the next chapter, I'll explain how to tame and handle your new pet.

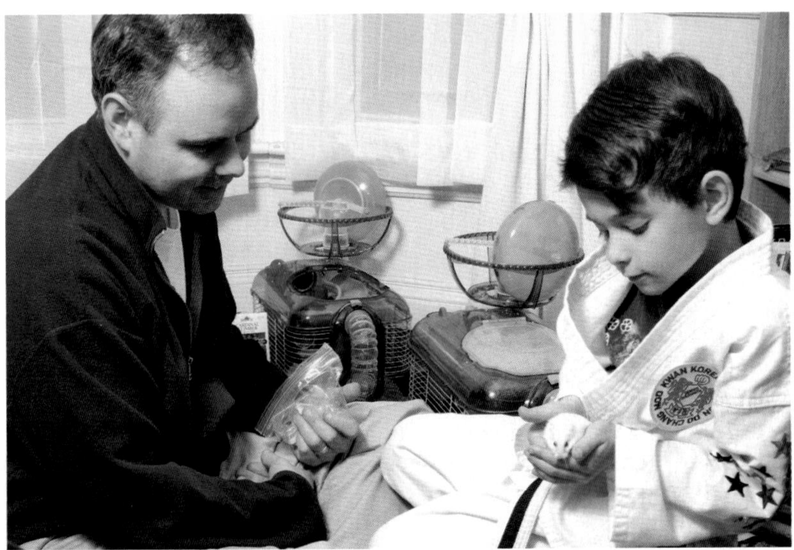

Make sure your hamster's habitat is all ready before you bring him home.

Chapter 6

Day-to-Day Care and Handling

Now that your hamster is home, she will need basic habitat care and feeding. She'll also need to spend time playing and interacting with you. Let's start with what you will need to do to keep her home safe and clean. Then it's on to the introductions.

Household Upkeep

Regardless of the particular housing style you have chosen for your hamster, your pet's home must be cleaned thoroughly and regularly. A clean cage will keep your hamster happy, active, and in good health.

First, soiled bedding should be removed every day from the enclosure. This is typically quite simple, because most hamsters will designate one specific corner of their enclosure as the bathroom. Simply remove the soiled material and you have done your job. Replace what you have removed with fresh bedding, as necessary. Your goal, you remember, is to maintain a layer of fresh, safe bedding within your hamster's home that is approximately three inches thick.

Uneaten food should also be removed each day, as well, which may prove a bit more of a challenge. It's not unusual for a hamster with excess food available to fill her ample cheek pouches and bury her treasure somewhere within the bedding, perhaps in her nest box or beneath a favorite toy. If your hamster has adopted this traditional hamster habit, try to find her cache, clean it out, and thus prevent a buildup of odor and bacteria from the natural decomposition of food.

Wash the food dishes every day in warm, soapy water. Rinse them thoroughly and make sure they are dry before you put them back in your hamster's home. Change the water in the bottle every day, and check the sipping tube daily, too, to make sure it remains functional and that the stopper is not leaking. When you clean the bottle, rinse it thoroughly to remove all traces of soap, and replace it with a new bottle when it becomes worn or too dirty.

> **TIP**
>
> Follow the same weekly cleaning routine for any tubes and tunnels you have set up as part of your hamster's play area, and the hamster ball, if she uses one. Everything she spends time in or with should be cleaned regularly.

In addition to daily maintenance, the bedding should be completely removed and replaced every week. When it comes time to do this, place the hamster in an established holding cage or box—a small, secure enclosure equipped with a bit of bedding and a toy or two, as well as some food for the hamster's comfort and solace (you can also use this holding cage for trips to the veterinarian or for family travels). As with the main enclosure, make sure the holding cage is clean and escape-proof.

With your hamster safely confined and out of the way, carry on with the cleaning. Remove all the items from the cage and clean everything with warm water and mild soap or detergent. Dispose of the old bedding from the enclosure,

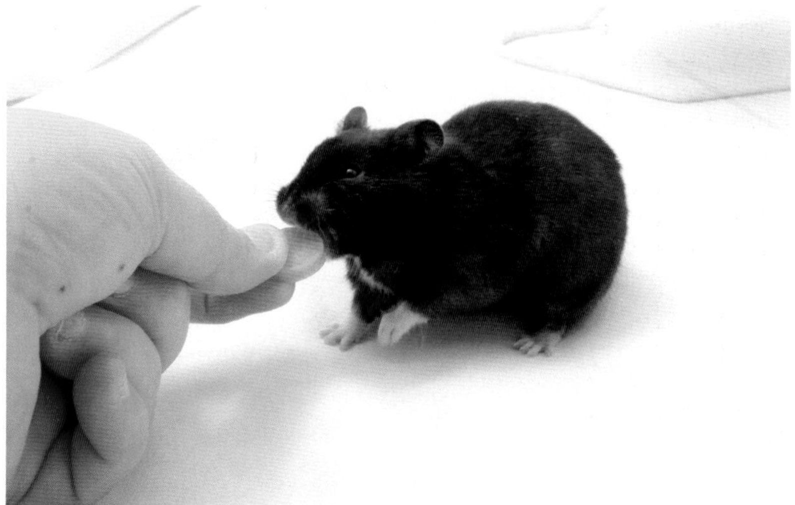

Offering a bit of food is a good way to start getting acquainted with your hamster.

and thoroughly clean the walls and the floor (or the bars of the cage) with warm water and mild soap. Avoid strong detergents or cleaning solvents that can irritate your pet's respiratory tract or prove to be toxic if they are not completely rinsed away. Rinse the soap from the enclosure thoroughly—you want to be rid of every bit of soap residue—and then dry the surfaces just as thoroughly before reintroducing your hamster to her abode.

Once the enclosure is dry, carpet the floor with a new, fresh three-inch layer of bedding, replace the cage furnishings, and, finally, welcome your hamster back into her home, sweet home.

Hamster Grooming

Because your hamster spends so much time grooming herself, it may be tempting to try to help her with the process. Please resist the temptation. Your hamster is perfectly capable of taking care of her own grooming requirements—no doubt a skill sculpted by her solitary life in the wild, where, in the absence of other hamsters to join in sessions of mutual grooming, the hamster learned to groom on her own. This has more to do with survival than with vanity, because a healthy coat is critical to protecting the hamster from climactic extremes.

Hamsters groom themselves, but the longhaired ones may need light brushing.

Hamsters Need Veterinary Care, Too!

From their own surveys of pet owners, the American Veterinary Medical Association has found that only a small percentage of hamster owners seek veterinary care for their pets, and that's a shame. All pets, from the tiniest mouse or frog to the most expensive champion show dog, should receive veterinary attention when they need it. This is simply another element of the grand commitment that is pet ownership.

Hamsters have a relatively short life span. Still, when we become owners we commit to all aspects of their care, including their medical care. In keeping with this philosophy, there are more veterinarians today who are experienced in the care of small and exotic animals, and more opportunities for hamster owners to seek help when their hamsters need it. To promote this very compassionate idea, some veterinarians even offer discounts to people who come to them with small animals in need of treatment.

When you are preparing for your new hamster pet, find a veterinarian in your area who is qualified to treat these tiny animals and takes that responsibility seriously. Odds are you will need the services of this practitioner at some point, and it is wise to have the number handy when you do.

Still, hamsters often appear to have a coat full of cage bedding or litter. They are, after all, little balls of nocturnal energy. You can help your pet remove this by simply "petting off" the particles. Or you can satisfy your desire to groom your little pet through short brushing sessions with a soft toothbrush. While this is not critical to hamster health and beauty, it does not harm your pet, and it offers you a chance to share some quality time with her.

At the same time, and perhaps more important, short brushing sessions give you the opportunity to observe your pet more closely for signs of any new or developing physical changes that could indicate illness or injury. For instance, while running the soft brush over the hamster's tummy, you may notice a lump that wasn't there before, or spot a damp area on her rear end that could signal the serious hamster illness known as wet tail. Contact the veterinarian right away, before a potentially serious condition progresses to perhaps untreatable stages.

As a rule, hamsters should not be bathed. Because their grooming routines (coupled with a habitat that is kept clean and pristine) cleanse them naturally, and because hamsters are essentially odorless by nature, there is no need for a human-style bath with soap and water. In addition to being unnecessary, bathing is extremely stressful for a hamster. Hamsters are especially prone to respiratory problems, so it is also best to avoid the chill a bath can cause.

For the record, you do not need to trim your pet's tiny toenails, either. In fact, you must not, because you can severely injure the little darling. If your hamster is having a problem with her feet, leave it to the veterinarian to handle.

Gentle Hamster Handling

Hamsters navigate their world by relying on their senses of smell and hearing. During your first few days together, let your pet get acquainted with your voice and your scent. Speak softly to your hamster when you approach her enclosure for daily feedings, water changes, toy rotations, and removing soiled bedding every day.

All family members can introduce themselves this way, but in the beginning try to keep interactions brief and to a minimum. And limit this contact to just the hamster's family members. The kids may be tempted to invite everyone in the neighborhood over to meet the family's new addition, but explain that it's better to wait a few days to let her adjust. Once you build that important foundation of respect, the hamster is more likely to be amenable to meeting outsiders.

When you believe the hamster is ready for you to do so—a positive sign is her noticeably calm demeanor and even courageous curiosity when your hand enters her habitat for daily maintenance—gently reach your hand into her habitat and leave it there, still and outstretched, an act that will invite the animal to approach and sniff your skin. If treated gently, most hamsters are not biters by nature. If your new pet does approach your hand but tries to take a little nip of your finger while exploring your skin, either she isn't ready for such an intrusion or perhaps she has caught a whiff of your lunch lingering on your fingertips.

You will further earn your hamster's esteem by carrying out these initial interactions in the late afternoon and early evening, when this nocturnal creature shakes off her daytime sleepiness and emerges energetic and ready for activity. If you awaken the animal constantly during the day when she is trying to sleep, she

How to Tame Your New Companion

It can take a while to get to know your new hamster pet, and even longer—days, weeks, even a month or two—for her to get to know you. But proceed patiently and gently, and you will finally see your tiny pet wiggle with delight whenever she hears your voice or catches your scent in the air. (Taming, remember, is an ongoing process with dwarf hamsters.)

1. Get to know your new pet. Is she a shy or gregarious golden, or an active winter white dwarf easily distracted by food? Whatever you learn about your pet will provide you with clues as to how she can be handled and tamed.
2. Make sure the room your hamster is in is quiet and still when you do the taming exercises described here.
3. Help your hamster grow accustomed to your voice. Speak softly to her when you place her meals in her enclosure and remove soiled bedding each day.
4. Help your hamster grow accustomed to your scent. Regularly place your hand into your hamster's enclosure and hold it still. Allow her to approach and sniff your skin. If she decides not to approach this time, try again later.
5. Once your hamster is familiar with your scent and, ideally, is willing to come to your hand, place a treat in your palm and hold that out to your pet in her enclosure. This extra incentive may also help inspire the hesitant hamster who has previously refused to approach your hand.
6. When your hamster will take the treat from your hand, she may eventually hop into your hand. Regardless of what progress you are making, remain patient, still, and soft-spoken. Repeat each successful step for several days to lock in your pet's trust.
7. Read your pet's signals so you can tell when she is comfortable with the current step and ready to move on. If, for example, your hamster climbs on your hand and doesn't want to leave, and repeats this for several days, you'll know you are ready for the next step.
8. When your hamster is comfortable in your hand within the cage, try lifting her out of the cage, supporting her with one hand under her and one over her back. She may be comfortable in your hand right away, even content crawling from one hand to the other as she revels in your scent and slow movements. Or she may take longer to adjust to each new sensation of hand-to-hamster contact, and that's okay, too.

Creative Hamster Holding

If your hamster is not the most cooperative animal when it's time to lift and hold her, try these methods:

- If you are unaccustomed to holding a hamster, you can take advantage of your pet's curiosity by holding a small box or plastic cup in front of her. Place a treat inside for an extra incentive. Your hamster will most likely venture inside the container to check it out, and you can then pick her up in the container.
- Scoop the hamster up, one hand holding her securely underneath her body, the other hand held over her back to create a "roof" that essentially hides the hamster safely within your hands.
- If your hamster loves to speed around the cage, darting playfully out of your grasp, create a wall by linking your open palms together side by side. Your pet will probably run into your open-palmed wall at some point, permitting you to close your hands gently around her body.

will likely become frustrated with this new, and rather inconsiderate, human in her life. Waking a soundly sleeping hamster, even one known for a docile disposition, could invite a bite that must not be blamed on hamster nastiness, but on owner negligence and disrespect.

Holding Your Hamster

After those first few days of quiet introductions, your hamster is ready for the next step: being held and carried. Proceed gradually. Before lifting the hamster out of her enclosure, speak softly to alert her to your presence. Next, gently place your hand into her enclosure as she has become accustomed to you doing.

When approaching your hamster, consider your own safety. Leave your hamster alone if she rolls over on her back and shows her teeth. This is a signal that

To prevent falls, make sure your kids hold the hamster over a table or near the floor, and never leave the hamster alone on the floor. Children definitely need to be supervised while holding the hamster.

she is feeling defensive or threatened. You should also respect her space if she runs from your hand or makes a squealing or guttural sound. Also remember to leave a sleeping hamster to her nap instead of waking her. Most of all, never squeeze, pinch, or handle your hamster in a rough manner.

While technically a hamster can be lifted by the excess skin at the nape of her neck, it is better to wrap your fingers gently yet firmly around her barrel-shaped little body to lift her. Use your other hand to offer extra support at the hamster's rear end, and hold the animal close to your body.

During initial outings and whenever children handle the hamster, make sure she is held over a nearby horizontal surface, such as a table or the floor, to prevent injuries if she falls. By the same token, never leave the hamster alone on a table or an elevated surface. This will invite disaster for your pet, who, due to her insatiable curiosity, could fall and be seriously injured.

Handling your hamster with respect and a quiet demeanor will instill in her a sense of security and a positive association with being handled. It will also help increase her affection for her new human family members. Your pet will recognize when she is being treated with respect and will quickly learn whom she can trust. Introduce yourself gradually and gently, observe preliminary safety precautions when handling your pet, and you will earn a reputation for being trustworthy.

Chapter 7

Feeding Your Hamster

The fact that it's so easy to provide a hamster with a healthy, well-balanced diet is yet another reason why this animal is celebrated as such an easy-care pet. He requires access to his food at all times, but supplying that food is so simple that even a young child can take on the duty (with regular parental supervision, of course).

Whatever you choose to feed your pet, make sure your pet has access to dry food and water throughout the day and evening. Hamsters love to snack, especially between naps, and they need frequent infusions of nutrients to fuel their speedy metabolisms. This is especially true of the dwarfs.

Nutritional Needs

Whether you choose to live with a golden hamster or one (or more) of his smaller dwarf cousins, the nutritional requirements are the same. The metabolism of the dwarfs tends to be speedier than that of the larger goldens, but both types of hamsters require the same basic nutrients, the same basic diets, and the same basic feeding routines. In short, both must have good, fresh food available to them in the proper balance at all times, and both must be offered that fresh food every day.

Look to your pet's elusive wild cousins for clues as to what your domestic companion needs and enjoys. For instance, while we are inclined to think of the hamster as the quintessential vegetarian, hamsters in the wild enjoy quite a varied—and omnivorous—diet. In addition to feasting on the vegetation products he finds during his nightly forays into the desert, he may supplement his diet with insects and any other meat-based items he happens to find. In fact, when you look to that wild creature's eating habits, you are likely to realize that his ideal, well-balanced diet isn't that much different from your own.

Like all mammals, the hamster requires a balanced diet composed of a variety of basic nutrients: carbohydrates, fats, proteins, vitamins, minerals, and plenty of fresh, clean water. The most efficient way to supply your pet with these nutrients is with a diet that combines high-quality, commercially prepared hamster foods from the pet supply store with fresh foods from your own kitchen.

A Devout Vegetarian?

The answer to this question is rather simple: It depends.

A hamster's daily diet should be about 15 to 20 percent protein. That much is clear. Your job is to determine how the hamster gets that protein. You see, that vegetarian reputation helped attract many would-be hamster owners to these animals in the first place. Other owners are more tuned in to their hamster's wild origins, and don't mind them showing a little bit of their animal nature. These hamster keepers hold to the idea that you can best supplement the animal's diet with live mealworms. A somewhat safer and certainly easier method of supplying hamsters with animal-based protein is to offer them a bit of cooked meat from time to time.

Your hamster is basically a vegetarian, and a variety of fresh fruits and vegetables will greatly enhance his diet.

Feeding Your Hamster

Feeding your hamster is a simple task. Just follow these guidelines and ask your veterinarian if you have any concerns:

- Supply a varied diet consisting of a mix of commercially prepared food, fresh vegetables, and, occasionally, fruits.
- Keep fresh food available to your hamster at all times.
- Provide your pet with a constant supply of fresh, clean water.
- Offer healthy treats in moderation.

Neither of these practices is necessary, however, and they can actually cause digestive problems for the species that far outweigh any nutritional benefits. The nutritional benefits of mealworms, in particular, can be garnered far more easily from other food sources. This should come as good news to those who would rather not find—or smell—insect parts or less-than-fresh meat products hidden away within their pets' bedding.

The bottom line is this: Your small pet will live just as healthfully and comfortably without animal protein, as long as you take care to meet his general protein needs. Feel free to offer your hamster a basically vegetarian diet, but be sure to vary what you feed him. If you don't wish to give him meat, you can provide protein by occasionally feeding him milk products. A teaspoon of yogurt or cottage cheese mixed with fruit, for example, is a healthy alternative, but remember to wait until the food is at room temperature before feeding it, and make sure it is fresh. Provide small portions to avoid spoilage, and remove as soon as possible whatever your pet does not eat.

Commercial Diets

Thanks to the popularity of pocket pets and the growing body of knowledge about their nutritional needs, there are a variety of commercial products on the market that please both the hamster's palate and your desire for convenient feeds.

Basic seed mixtures are the most traditional of the commercially prepared foods. Most hamsters are thrilled with a mix of seeds, but seeds alone usually are not enough. Even if the seed mixture constitutes a nutritionally balanced diet, many hamsters pick and choose and do not eat all the types of seeds within the mix. It's not at all unusual for a particularly finicky hamster to choose to feast only on sunflower seeds or only on some other favored type of seed he finds in the mixture. Because no one food, especially no one seed, is the perfect food, eating this way will lead to malnutrition.

Seeds and nuts are also very high in fat, and an excess can lead to obesity. In moderation, they are proper components of the hamster's diet, but they are not appropriate as the only components.

Pelleted or block-type commercial diets prevent the problems of the seed mixture. Combined within the pellets and blocks are all the nutrients the hamster requires for a complete and balanced diet—none of which can be picked out and rejected. Many of the block diets present an added bonus: Their hard consistency helps keep those hamster teeth trimmed, maintaining the animal's dental health while nourishing him at the same time.

Because the seed mixture is generally tastier and more interesting to a hamster than the pelleted and block-type food, it's wise to offer both to ensure the hamster enjoys his meal and gets a proper mix of nutrients. If you happen to have a hamster who prefers seeds, however, you may need to wait to offer the seed mixture until after the hamster has eaten a ration of pellets or blocks.

In addition to providing a hamster with complete nutrition, commercial diets have the added convenience of being readily available at most pet supply stores, and they can be easily stored. Resist the temptation to stock up on these foods, however, because even though they have a relatively long shelf life, they can still go bad. When purchased in modest amounts and stored

Seed mixtures are a popular commercial diet. They are fine for your hamster, but only as part of a more varied diet.

Foods to Avoid

While feeding hamsters can be fun (a nibbling hamster is adorable), steer clear of the following food items:

- Canned and frozen vegetables
- Uncooked beans
- The green parts of potatoes and tomatoes
- Sprouting potatoes
- Fried foods
- Table scraps and leftovers from your own table
- Sweets of any kind

correctly—preferably, in airtight plastic containers with secure lids—commercial hamster food should remain fresh and clean for weeks. If, however, you notice the food has become moldy, stale, or otherwise less than ideal, do not offer it to your hamster. Throw it all away and buy a fresh batch.

Keep It Fresh

Feeding your hamster a few tiny bites of fresh food each day helps to round out the diet and to keep the hamster interested in eating. Most hamsters love nothing more than to go to the food dish and find a small helping of chopped fresh vegetables, such as broccoli, parsley, carrots, or perhaps a couple of peas. Tiny chunks of cheese, cooked pasta, or whole wheat bread, and an occasional morsel of apple or orange, can also be added to the diet.

Make sure you provide only the freshest, highest-quality items that are properly and thoroughly cleaned and rinsed. These foods, fed sparingly, must be of the same quality you would demand for your own diet. Feeding him leftovers, table scraps, or any type of "junk" food (even if such a food is something he adores) could result in gastric upset and obesity.

Remember that even the freshest of foods won't stay that way for long, so the uneaten portions must be removed each day to prevent spoilage. Keep track of what fresh foods you offer your pet, and how much you feed him, because your hamster may spirit these fresh foods away to his hidden supply—where many a hamster is apt to deliver the leftovers. If the daily ration seems to have disappeared

A little bite of a fresh strawberry can be a tasty treat.

too quickly, search for a stash of food within his housing structures or bedding, because it will spoil quickly and create a health (and odor) hazard.

The All-Important Extras

Hamsters need not live by a balance sheet of nutrients alone. They can, and should, enjoy a treat from time to time. Treats should be healthy and must be offered to your pet in moderation. Appropriate and highly coveted hamster treats include raisins, peanuts in the shell, a small bite of fruit, and various commercially prepared treats that contain a variety of natural ingredients.

Regardless of what type of treats you choose, they must be offered sparingly so as not to interfere with the balance of the hamster's primary diet or cause gastric upset or obesity. As their name implies, offering treats should not be viewed as an everyday event, nor should they be considered

TIP

One way to find an escaped and soon-to-be-hungry hamster is to entice him out into the open by baiting each room with his favorite treats. After setting out your bait—say, a handful of raisins—in every room of the house—you may find yourself walking into a room where you least expect to spot the hamster, and find him sitting up on his haunches, nibbling contentedly on a raisin he holds securely in his delicate hands.

Safe and Nutritious Foods

As we have seen, the wise hamster caretaker supplements their pet's daily commercial diet with fresh foods that are not only palatable, but that also contribute to this tiny animal's daily nutritional needs. Here is a list of food options that, in moderation, you can safely and confidently feed your hamster.

Apples
Bananas
Blueberries
Carrots
Cauliflower
Chicken
Corn (cob to gnaw on)
Cottage cheese
Dandelion leaves
Dog biscuits
Eggs (cooked)
Fish (cooked)
Grapes
Lettuce (iceberg)
Meadow hay
Mealworms
Meat (cooked)
Pasta (cooked)
Potatoes (cooked or raw)
Raspberries
Rice (boiled)
Sprouts
Strawberries
Sunflower seeds
Tomatoes
White bread
Yogurt

part of the basic diet, although they should be healthy in that they help contribute to the hamster's daily nutritional requirements.

And finally, don't forget water, a vital hamster nutrient and the one component that binds all the others together. Without fresh, clean water every day, the hamster's system—or any mammal's—will be completely unable to operate. Each and every cell within the body requires water to function and to reproduce.

It is no surprise that without ample amounts of water in his system, an animal's blood cannot flow correctly, his organs cannot do their jobs, and his brain cannot function as it should. A lack of water (typically caused either by an empty water bottle or dish, an illness that causes a hamster not to drink, or stress or diarrhea) leads to dehydration, which may lead to death. This can easily be prevented, of course, by supplying your small pet with fresh, clean water in squeaky clean containers every day—and monitoring how much he drinks.

How to Feed a Hamster

Once you understand the simple components of the optimum hamster diet, which really are not all that different from those of your own balanced diet, you must design a feeding schedule that will enhance your tiny pet's health. Just as you did when deciding what to feed him, here too, all you need to do is look to the example set by his wild ancestors.

This example can be summed up in three simple words: freshness, variety, quality. Make sure every morsel of food you offer your pet is something that contributes to his daily nutritional requirements—perhaps even something that you wouldn't mind eating yourself (minus the mealworms and the hamster chow, of course). You thus take an important step toward ensuring that your pet lives as long, as healthfully, and as comfortably as he possibly can.

The next step is to determine just how you should offer these foods to your pet. As we have seen, your hamster is a rodent with a speedy metabolism and must have access to food at all times to satisfy those ample energy needs. Although the hamster will typically eat most of his food during the night, he must have food available during the day as well, in case he awakens and needs a midday snack. Your job is to make sure that when he feels hunger pangs, day or night, he finds the feast he is seeking in a clean, accessible location.

Consider Those Rainy Days

The wild hamster has more to tell you about how to feed your little pet. Remember that whether in the wild or housed in a domestically designed aquarium-style domain, the hamster is a keen believer in the idea of saving for a rainy day. In other words, he will munch happily on the food you feed him, but he will also feel the need to hide, or cache, some of that food, sometimes in his cheeks, but more commonly in his bedding.

Many a hamster keeper has thus discovered that feeding from a regular feeding dish can help facilitate this small animal's natural impulses and keep the cage clean at the same time. That's because some hamsters come to view their food dishes as nice, secure caches that have been oh-so-conveniently and generously built in to their homes. These hamsters thus feel no inclination to hide their food elsewhere.

If, however, you find that your little friend would rather choose his own hiding places, you will need to remain vigilant in your cleaning, changing, and investigating of the bedding to prevent spoilage and odor.

Feeding Dishes and More

Regardless of your particular pet's caching preferences, if you plan to feed your hamster with a traditional feeding dish, the best choice is a heavy ceramic bowl. This bowl should be weighted at the bottom to prevent your pet from tipping it over in the throes of a feeding frenzy and leaving a mess of food on the cage floor and bedding. To protect that floor further, nest the dish securely within the bedding to prevent spillage.

Place the dish a good distance from the hamster's nest box and away from his designated bathroom area as well. In the fastidious little hamster's mind, there must be a distinct place for everything and everything must be in its place, with proper distance between "rooms." Take this seriously and plan accordingly. A chaotic home design will only lead to life-threatening stress and confusion in your small pet.

If you have a problem with the hamster soiling his food in an open-air dish situated in the middle of the enclosure—common with a hamster whose favorite place to sit is inside his food dish—there are dish styles available that can clamp on to your pet's cage wall. Such a dish must, of course, sit low enough to the floor of the habitat to make it easily accessible to the hamster—very low for the dwarfs.

Hamsters tend to stash their uneaten food, so be sure to search your pet's bedding and remove the leftovers before they start to spoil.

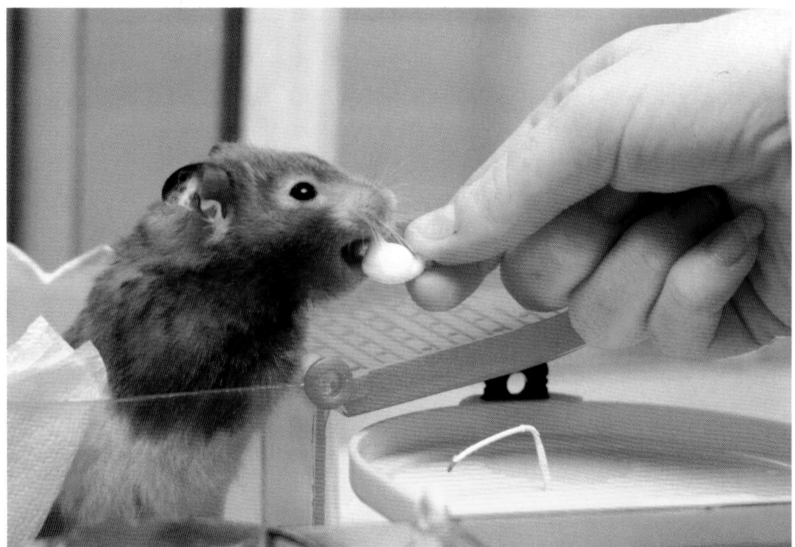

Every inch of your hamster's habitat needs to be clean all the time. That includes all his play areas; make sure he eats what you offer him, or throw it away.

Another option is a block-type diet administered from receptacles that hang from an enclosure wall. These must also, of course, be placed low enough for the hamster to reach. Of course, you'll still need food dishes for the seed mixture, if it is being offered, and any fresh foods the hamster will be eating that day.

Water Containers

As one of the most important components of the hamster diet, fresh water must be offered to your hamster each day, preferably in a water bottle with a metal sipping tube mounted on the side of the enclosure. (Avoid water bottles with plastic tubes that can be chewed and destroyed by a hamster's gnawing.) The bottle should be emptied and refilled daily with a fresh supply of water, and the sipping tube must be checked every day, too, for possible blockages that would prevent the hamster from drinking properly and getting the fluid his body needs.

You might also offer water in a heavy ceramic dish identical to the type of dish you use for food, but this is a far messier alternative and is not ideal for hamsters. Aside from the fact that the water in the dish can become soiled with food, dust, bedding, and feces, there is also the danger that the water will spill, leaving the hamster without drinking water and a habitat floor carpeted with soaked bedding.

Clean, Clean, Clean

Knowing the hamster and his need for cleanliness as you do by now, regardless of the equipment with which you choose to feed and water your hamster, all items must be cleaned thoroughly each day. Empty the previous day's contents (food or water), scrub the dish or bottle with a mild soap and warm water (avoid strong detergents and chemical disinfectants), and rinse the item thoroughly to remove all soap residue. If soap remains on the dish or bottle, the hamster could ingest it with his next meal or drink, and subsequently suffer from a nasty bout of gastric upset.

After cleaning, place these furnishings back in their familiar locations, complete with fresh servings of food and water, and your hamster will be as grateful for your efforts as he is for the food—whether he quite realizes this or not.

Chapter 8

Keeping Your Hamster Healthy

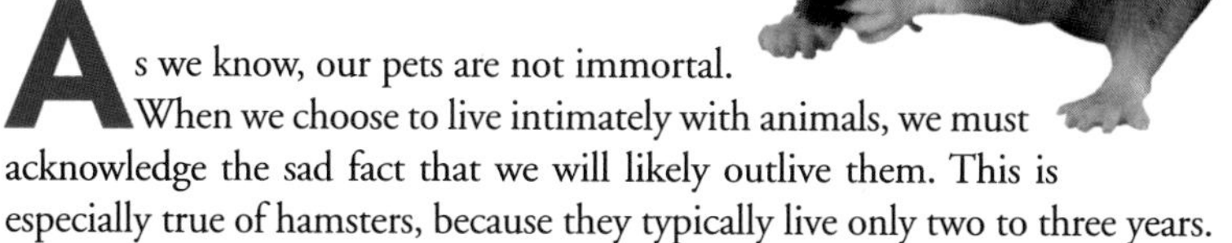

As we know, our pets are not immortal. When we choose to live intimately with animals, we must acknowledge the sad fact that we will likely outlive them. This is especially true of hamsters, because they typically live only two to three years.

But although their life spans are short, we are honor bound to do all we can to make those years as fulfilling and healthy as possible for these tiny animals, and to alleviate any suffering they may have. Toward this end, there are steps we can take to help them enjoy the longest lives possible and to foster the lovely bond that can exist between human and hamster.

Preventive Care

The first step in your mission as guardian of your hamster's health is to get to know your pet well, and then to observe her carefully and regularly for subtle changes that could indicate the early stages of a health problem. The medical establishment has long understood that the earlier treatment is sought for an ailment, the greater chance the patient of any species has of recovering successfully. It is thus up to you, the person who knows your hamster best, to look for those early signs.

It's so simple. Get to know your pet's physical and behavioral characteristics when she is healthy: the texture and density of her hair; the contour of her skin and physique; the patterns of her eating, sleeping, and playing behaviors; and her natural aroma. Armed with this information, you will be better prepared to notice any change that could indicate the first sign of a problem. Early treatment and fast action will increase the opportunity for a full recovery.

Hamster Warning Signs

Signs of Common Illness

These signs could indicate a number of conditions that require veterinary attention:

- Sudden onset of uncharacteristic lethargy (especially at playtime in the late afternoon and evening)
- Lack of appetite
- Deterioration in the quality, density, and texture of the hair (remember that some loss and thinning of hair is common as a hamster ages)
- Swollen abdomen
- Incessant scratching
- Failure to tend to routine grooming duties
- An unusual odor from what is essentially an odorless animal

Signs of Serious Illness

You should also be on the lookout for more complex behaviors and symptoms that can indicate a more serious condition. All of these require prompt veterinary attention:

- Diarrhea and/or moisture around the hamster's rear end (the classic signs of wet tail, see page 86)
- Circling behavior (possible ear infection)
- Excessive thirst and urination (signs that can indicate kidney disease, diabetes, or adrenal disease)
- Lumps or bumps under the skin (could signal tumors or abscesses)
- Discharge from the eyes (possible eye infection)

Practicing Prevention

While careful observation is critical, you can further protect this tiny animal's health—and prevent problems—by adopting responsible hamsterkeeping practices, as outlined in chapters 6 and 7. A balanced diet of only the highest-quality ingredients, combined with a clean, dry enclosure positioned in a quiet spot, away from drafts and direct sunlight, are the best ways you have to keep you hamster healthy—and to help her recover from an illness.

Your hamster's stress levels should also be kept to a minimum, because stress is one of the primary contributors to the deterioration of hamster health. While stress itself is not a disease, its presence in a hamster's life undermines the tiny animal's immune system and opens the door to bacteria and viruses that can harm her.

Keep your hamster healthy by keeping her habitat clean. That includes her cage and all her toys, tubes, and tunnels.

Keep stress under control by sticking to a regular routine in your hamster's daily and weekly care and by keeping her habitat clean and well-maintained. In addition, restrict her interactions only to those individuals who respect the hamster and understand how to handle her correctly (the family cat or dog is probably not one of these).

Housing a golden hamster alone or a dwarf with a trusted (and very healthy) buddy in a clean, quiet, properly appointed abode is also important in keeping stress low and preserving hamster health.

Keeping Quarantine

Quarantine can be another valuable prevention tool. It is wise when bringing a new hamster into the household to quarantine her for a few weeks to ensure she doesn't bring in contagious illnesses that might infect existing hamster residents. And when I say quarantine, I mean it. The newcomer should have her own habitat, and that habitat should be kept in a separate room during those first weeks. Some illnesses are spread by airborne transmission, so a more formal quarantine is necessary to ensure that all of the hamsters of the household are healthy and present no danger to each other.

It goes without saying, then, that a new hamster, for her own safety as well as that of your other pets, should never be brought home and simply placed into an existing hamster's habitat, even if, for example, a new dwarf is destined ultimately to share her digs with another resident.

As Your Hamster Ages

Even the most diligent adherence to preventive measures cannot grant a pet hamster immortality, or even immunity from disease. After her first or second birthday, you will begin to notice some changes in your pet that are common to aging hamsters. These include some hair loss, a dip in energy levels, and some subtle changes in her daily routine. If your are observant and have come to know your pet well, you will recognize when a change, even a minor one, calls for medical attention.

Common Hamster Health Problems

Hamsters are prone to a variety of health problems, many of which can be prevented or treated more successfully if the animals are cared for by observant, well-informed owners. Educate yourself about these conditions, keep stress in your pet's life to a minimum, and maintain a clean, safe, warm, dry environment for your hamster, and you will prepare your pet to combat the problems that can threaten her health.

Allergies

Allergies are not all that uncommon in the hamster family. Some hamsters are allergic to certain foods; others to types of bedding; and others to strong odors or chemicals in their environment, such as cleaning agents, cologne, or cigarette smoke. If your hamster is sneezing and her eyes are watering, yet her behavior has not changed, you probably have a hamster with an allergy. Other possible signs of allergy include redness of the feet; dry, flaky, itchy skin; and/or hair loss.

Treatment depends on the specific allergy, so, if possible, try to determine what might be causing the problem. Try feeding your hamster a simple diet with just a single protein source to pinpoint a food allergy. Easily digestible foods such as white rice and white bread, fruits and vegetables, and cereal (such as cornflakes) can help determine if food is the culprit.

If this doesn't work, try changing your hamster's bedding. She may be allergic to the filler (such as sawdust). If bedding dust and oils are your pet's problem, try a pelleted paper or vegetable product, and avoid cedar and wood shavings.

Alleviating your hamster's allergy-related breathing difficulties or skin reactions by altering problem-causing agents within her environment is not only simple, but it can also result in quick and noticeable improvement.

Bleeding

Bleeding can be a sign of cancer, problems with digestive organs, or a prolapsed rectum (bleeding from the rectum is especially serious because it can be a sign of tumors, cancer, ulcers, or intestinal problems), or it can be caused by an external injury to the hamster. This can be something as minor as a superficial cut on a leg from an exposed wire in the cage, a foot injury from an overzealous run on the wheel, or something as severe as a bite wound from a fellow hamster who objects to sharing a habitat.

Any type of bleeding warrants an immediate call to the veterinarian for advice on how the patient's particular case should be handled. Your pet may require on-site veterinary attention to stop the bleeding, or simple nursing care at home involving, for example, the application of hydrogen peroxide or Betadine on a cotton swab to keep the wound clean and free from infection.

Follow the veterinarian's advice exactly on how to deal with the wound, even with treatment as seemingly simple as the choice of topical antibiotic ointments or similar medications. Some preparations can be absorbed into the hamster's system through the skin and prove to be toxic. This problem may be exacerbated if the hamster licks at the wound, thus taking even more of the substance into her system.

Hamsters may be allergic to their bedding. If you see signs of allergies, try switching to a paper or vegetable bedding product.

Colds

Just like humans, hamsters are susceptible to colds and can actually catch colds from you. In addition to minimizing your own hand-to-paw contact with your pet when you have a cold or the flu, a good preventive measure is to keep your hamster away from drafts, moisture, and severe drops in temperature; she needs moderate temperatures at all times.

If your hamster has a runny nose and watery eyes; if she is sneezing, lethargic, and having trouble breathing; if she's not all that interested in eating and you find her curled up in a corner refusing your invitations to play, she most likely has a cold or other type of respiratory infection. Be warned: This is nothing for you to sneeze at. A cold in a hamster can quickly turn into life-threatening pneumonia. She must be treated immediately and diligently.

First, place your pet's cage in a warm area that is free from drafts and damp air. Carpet her home with thick layers of clean, fresh, safe bedding (in other words, no cedar or pine) for extra warmth and comfort. Your veterinarian should be notified about your pet's condition, because respiratory troubles can indicate a host of problems both internal (heart trouble) and external (chemicals in the environment) that may not be apparent at first glance. If the condition persists for two days, or takes a sudden turn for the worse, a personal visit to the vet is in order for your tiny pet.

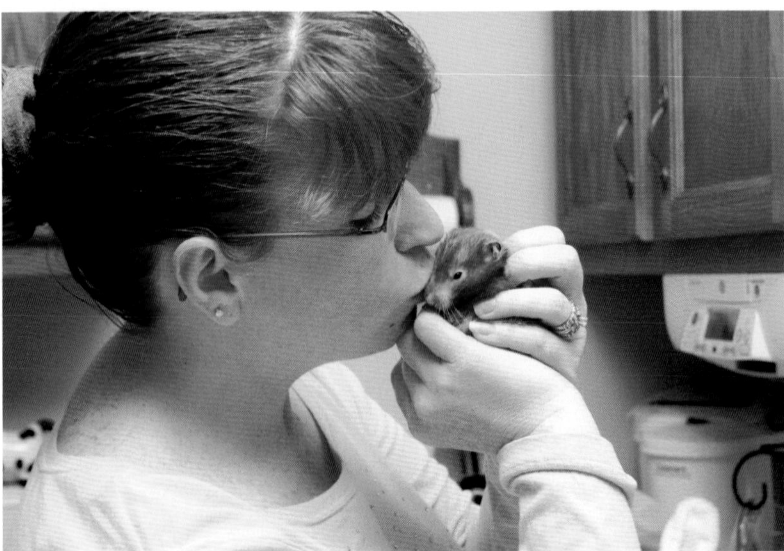

Hamsters can catch our colds. So if you're feeling under the weather, kissing is probably not a good idea.

Constipation

Your hamster should never be too cold or too hot. Both can be dangerous.

Symptoms of constipation in a hamster are a distended (enlarged) belly, lethargy, and arching of the back. The animal will probably prefer not to be held or petted because of her great discomfort. A lack of exercise and a diet lacking in fresh fruits and vegetables can cause constipation, and your hamster may be so uncomfortable that she does not want to eat at all.

In that case, you can use an eyedropper to give her a few drops of olive oil, which can be very effective in clearing up the condition. As your hamster begins feeling better, give her plenty of moisture-rich greens, such as lettuce, and some juicy fruits—but not too much, or you will be faced with the next condition.

Diarrhea

Diarrhea is a classic sign of the potentially fatal hamster condition wet tail (see page 86), but it can signal other problems as well, particularly when a hamster is not getting a properly balanced diet.

Feeding your hamster green vegetables, for example, is important, but you don't want to overfeed these items or suddenly change your pet's diet. Make this mistake and you will find yourself faced with a very messy hamster cage and an equally messy occupant of that cage, due to those loose droppings. A quick call to the veterinarian will help to determine whether the condition is food-related or something more serious. If diet is to blame, try offering your pet only dry food for a while, which will usually help her quickly recover. Once you have reversed the problem, you can slowly reintroduce green foods into the diet, but in more moderate amounts this time.

Do not automatically assume diarrhea is simply a sign of a dietary problem. It can indicate something far more serious, so if it persists, or if changes in diet fail to clear up the problem, call the veterinarian.

Heatstroke

Hamsters tend to thrive best in mild temperatures, somewhere between 65 and 80 degrees Fahrenheit, but your pet's cage must not be kept in direct sunlight or

How to Handle Wet Tail

Perhaps the most prevalent, most dreaded disease in the pet hamster population is the condition we call wet tail, scientifically known as *proliferative ileitis*. Highly contagious, this is a bacterial infection that causes severe diarrhea in a hamster and often proves to be fatal. The following guidelines will help you to recognize the disease and perhaps even save your hamster's life.

1. Educate yourself about the disease. Wet tail is more common in golden hamsters than in dwarfs, and it most commonly strikes newly acquired pets who have just recently left their mothers and been thrust into a new, unfamiliar environment. The ability of the bacteria that causes the condition to gain a foothold in the hamster is directly linked to conditions within the animal's environment that make her system susceptible to bacterial infection.

Stress, for example, is considered an important factor in the proliferation of wet tail (and explains why the disease is so prevalent in young hamsters during their early days in new homes). Sudden changes in diet, habitat overcrowding, extreme temperatures, and unsanitary living conditions also cause stress.

2. Watch for the signs. Wet tail is most often discovered in a household with new pets, the hamsters having contracted the disease at the pet shop or breeding facility. Although wet tail is most common in young weanling hamsters, it may affect older hamsters as well, so you should always watch for its symptoms—especially when new hamsters join the household.

The classic signs of wet tail are:

- Watery, usually pale, strong-smelling diarrhea, and, consequently, moisture around the hamster's tail (hence the name)
- Loss of appetite
- Dehydration
- A messy, unkempt coat
- Rectal bleeding or rectal prolapse
- Uncharacteristic irritability

Keep in mind that a wet rear end or even diarrhea alone do not automatically mean the hamster has wet tail. A wet tail can also be a sign of a nutritional imbalance, a bladder or uterine infection, or even an entirely different illness. No matter what the cause, wetness in the rear section is a symptom that should be evaluated by a veterinarian immediately—the sooner the better.

3. Seek treatment immediately. With immediate and proper intervention, wet tail can be treated successfully. First, if you even suspect your pet has been infected, isolate her immediately from any other hamsters you may have. Place her in a clean, warm, dry enclosure and call the veterinarian right away. Resist any temptation to treat your hamster with an over-the-counter product or with a "surefire" home remedy you find on the Internet. Treatment usually involves administering a combination of antibiotics, fluid therapy, and antidiarrheal medications. Since medicating a hamster is a delicate task, only the veterinarian should direct such treatment. Hamsters, for example, can have severe reactions to antibiotics, as well as to over-the-counter remedies that promise results.

Aside from following the veterinarian's treatment regimen, keep the sick hamster away from any healthy hamsters in the household, and keep her habitat clean, warm, and dry. Without proper care and consideration, the patient can just as likely succumb to the dehydration as to the disease itself. Indeed, the survival of a hamster with wet tail is directly linked to the quality of nursing she receives from you.

4. Prevent wet tail. Because of the highly contagious nature of the condition, keep new hamsters you are welcoming into your home quarantined during their first few weeks with you. It's also wise to make a habit of washing your hands thoroughly before and after handling any hamsters in your home.

Prevention basically rests in the fundamentals of responsible hamsterkeeping: a high-quality diet; fresh water; a clean, safe living space; pristine bedding that is changed regularly; and a stress-free hamster lifestyle. A commitment to good hamsterkeeping will help keep your hamster's tail clean and dry.

5. Preventive antibiotics? One controversial practice you may see promoted is preventing wet tail by routinely administering antibiotics to a new hamster, whether or not she exhibits any signs of disease. But antibiotics present their own threat to hamsters, so routine treatment of healthy hamsters may be dangerous. Treating a healthy hamster with antibiotics and without veterinary supervision may also cause drug resistance. This will cause the antibiotics to be ineffective if the hamster ever requires antibiotics in the future for an actual illness.

too close to a heat source, as this will lead to a dangerously overheated hamster. Also key to a safe body temperature is a supply of clean, easily accessible drinking water, which should be available to your hamster at all times.

If you happen to notice that your pet's fur is damp, she seems unresponsive, and you can't seem to prod her into an alert reaction to you, you may have a hamster with heatstroke. Speedy action is in order to save your pet's life. Begin cooling your hamster by dripping cool (*not cold*) water over her and urging her to drink. If she doesn't snap completely back to her fun and chipper self shortly, take her to the veterinarian.

Hair and Skin Problems

As the largest organ of the body, the skin, in concert with the hair, is a powerful indicator of problems on the surface, as well as what is going on inside a hamster.

Hair Loss

As your hamster ages, natural changes will occur in her skin and hair—a thinning or loss of hair, a thickening or blemishing of the skin, and similar changes. But there may be other explanations, too. Upon close examination of the hamster's daily activities, you may find, for example, that hair loss is being caused by your pet rubbing up against rough surfaces within her enclosure.

Pay close attention if your hamster starts losing her hair, because it could be a sign of illness.

Skin and hair changes should be closely monitored because they can indicate more serious health concerns. If, for example, hair loss is accompanied by a hamster's increased thirst, you are looking at the classic signs of adrenal disease, the treatment for which includes surgical removal of the adrenal gland(s). Other culprits include thyroid disease or, in females, disease of the reproductive tract.

Parasites

Hair loss and skin problems can also be caused by parasites. The most common parasites that effect hamsters are demodex mites, which cause demodectic mange. Mites are common and typically benign residents on hamsters, yet they can become a problem if the host hamster develops a more serious internal illness. That illness can open the door to a severe mite infestation, the successful treatment of which is curing the illness first, and then addressing the mites. As is the case for all serious conditions that afflict hamsters, forget the over-the-counter remedies and get the hamster to her veterinarian for treatment.

Abscesses and Tumors

The most common causes of lumps and bumps you may find on your hamster's skin are abscesses and tumors. Abscesses can be quite painful. They will sometimes open and drain on their own, but in most cases this must be done by the veterinarian. Tumors, too, may require surgical removal, depending on their type and where they are located on the hamster's body.

Scratching

Hamsters are meticulously clean little animals, but incessant, compulsive scratching is not part of the normal grooming program. The hamster driven to this may be suffering from a parasite infestation, adrenal disease, a fungal infection, liver disease, a dietary imbalance, or a lack of particular nutrients. Allergies to either food or elements in the environment (such as dusty or aromatic bedding, chemical disinfectants, or shampoos) can also cause abnormal scratching behavior. Locate the cause (with your veterinarian's help), and, with any luck, you can reverse this destructive and often painful behavior.

Tooth Problems

As a rodent, the hamster is no stranger to tooth problems. As would-be hamster owners learn while researching their pet of choice, rodent incisors grow constantly throughout the animals' lives. Natural gnawing and chewing keeps them trimmed, but if the jaw is somehow misshapen, injured, or infected, or the hamster is offered

Tooth care is extremely important for all rodents. Take your hamster to the veterinarian right away if you notice a lack of appetite, a bad odor from her head or mouth, drooling, breathing problems, or overgrown teeth.

an improper diet, the teeth can overgrow and lead to a host of painful problems and infections.

Signs of hamster tooth troubles include a lack of appetite, an unpleasant odor from the head and mouth, drooling, breathing problems, or outright deformity if overgrown teeth misalign the hamster's bite or even pierce the mouth.

The remedy may include antibiotic therapy, a change in diet, or regular manual trimming of the teeth. Indeed, like so many problems that can threaten our hamsters' health and contentment, teeth problems require professional veterinary attention, both to ensure correction of the problem and to alleviate the animal's pain and suffering.

Unexpected Pregnancy

As members of the rather prolific rodent family tree, there is no shortage of hamsters on the market. You'll discover this as soon as you go out to choose your hamster companion. Unfortunately, though, good, responsible, permanent homes for the many hamsters bred and born each year are not as plentiful. In light of this situation, unless you intend to keep the offspring for the duration of their lives, intentionally breeding your hamster is not a particularly responsible thing to do.

Some people believe they can make money breeding hamsters. Another motivation for breeding is to teach the kids "the miracle of life." Again, these ideas fail to take into account the well-being of the hamsters and the often insurmountable challenge of finding good, permanent homes for them.

If you are thinking about breeding your hamster, remember that you bought this animal for companionship. You brought her into your home so you could have the opportunity to coexist with a species so different from your own, to revel in how blessed we humans are to be able to adopt such creatures and live happily in their presence. She is not a source of income.

Unfortunately, though, many a well-meaning hamster owner ends up an inadvertent hamster breeder. This usually occurs at the beginning of the owner-hamster relationship, when, several weeks after bringing an adorable pair of allegedly female dwarf hamsters home, you discover that those two hamsters have become a family of seven, eight, maybe nine. If that happens to you, you will need a crash course in the care of that new little family, both to help the little ones survive and to prevent a repeat performance.

CAUTION

Releasing pet animals "into the wild" is not only cruel, it also wreaks havoc with native wildlife by interfering with their food chain and natural habitat. Domestic hamsters set loose in wild areas face starvation, injury, illness, and countless other dangers for which they are not prepared.

Breeding Basics

Hamsters boast one of the quickest reproduction rates in the animal kingdom. Reaching sexual maturity at about two months of age, hamster gestation is also phenomenally short—about sixteen days.

When kept in captivity as pets, hamsters are sometimes housed together. This is preferable for properly socialized dwarfs, while goldens instinctively prefer a solitary existence. The classic wild goldens typically come together with other hamsters only for breeding, after which they go their separate ways, leaving the females to raise their young as single mothers.

While breeders of dwarf hamsters have an easy time playing matchmaker, given the natural affection these critters have for each other, serious breeders of goldens tend to follow this same natural wild pattern—housing the male and female hamsters separately, placing a female in estrus with the designated male only at the opportune time, and watching the pair carefully for signs of incompatibility. A female who doesn't happen to be in the mood can be dangerous to the amorous male in her midst. If she isn't ready, it's best to keep the two apart until she is (and to remove the male after a successful mating has taken place).

About two weeks later, the female will be ready to give birth. In preparation, the breeder will clean her enclosure and replace the bedding, because Mom will remain undisturbed with her young for the first couple of weeks after they are born.

As her due date approaches, the mother-to-be will become restless. This is the signal that you should refrain from handling and playing with her. A day or two later, you will notice that, as if by magic, the enclosure now holds a new litter of five to ten naked babies.

Care of the Litter

Hamster mothers don't appreciate interference from humans, so the little family is best left alone for a week or two to prevent stress. If the mother feels stressed or threatened during those first couple of weeks, she may kill her young. Resist the temptation to get involved and let nature take its course.

As the weeks pass, the young hamsters will sprout hair, begin to share their mother's solid food (although they will not be completely weaned until they are almost a month old), and begin to venture farther away from Mom's side. Before you know it, they will look at the world with that cheeky, whimsical expression that sets the hamster apart from all other rodents and has made the species famous.

You are then faced with the challenge of placing the young animals into new and permanent homes. While siblings can usually coexist for awhile, you may have to separate them if placing them takes longer than you expected. And indeed, that is the hard part. The breeding is easy; the responsibility of placement is tough and not something the accidental breeder ever expects to have to deal with.

When faced with this responsibility, your best option is to contact your local animal shelter. Whether or not they are adopting out hamsters themselves, they may be able to refer people looking for hamster pets to you. You will then need to

Hamsters are not wild animals, and you cannot simply "release" unwanted babies into the wide world.

screen potential owners who are interested in your babies. Ask about their families, other pets, living situations, hamster knowledge, and so forth. Gauge their commitment to this little pet and be sure they are serious about the responsibility.

When It's Time to Say Good-Bye

Loving your hamster is an emotional investment with wonderful rewards. Unfortunately, though, the time will come when you will have to say good-bye to your tiny friend. If you're lucky, she will pass on as she sleeps. But you may reach the point where you will have to make the decision for her. Indeed, if your hamster is severely injured or extremely ill, you will do her a great act of kindness by making the tough decision to end her suffering with humane euthanasia performed by the veterinarian. One quick injection and the animal succumbs to a deep, quiet, endless sleep.

The decision to euthanize your pet is as difficult as it is personal. Your veterinarian can help you evaluate your pet's quality of life. Make sure you understand completely your pet's diagnosis and her degree of comfort, and take time to think through your decision. Once you have decided to euthanize your hamster, you may want to plan a special time for you and your family members to be alone with her and say a private good-bye.

Your veterinarian can help you keep your hamster healthy—and decide when her quality of life is greatly diminished.

Being honest about your emotions is the best way to start coping with the loss of your pet. It is normal to feel sad and experience feelings of loss. Once your hamster is gone, allow yourself time to grieve and accept that you will need time to adjust to your life without your little pet. Talk to friends and relatives, and remember that talking about your loss can help in the healing process. You will always have loving memories of the happy times you shared with your pet, and that relationship can serve to build a new one with a new hamster companion when you feel you are ready to take that step once more.

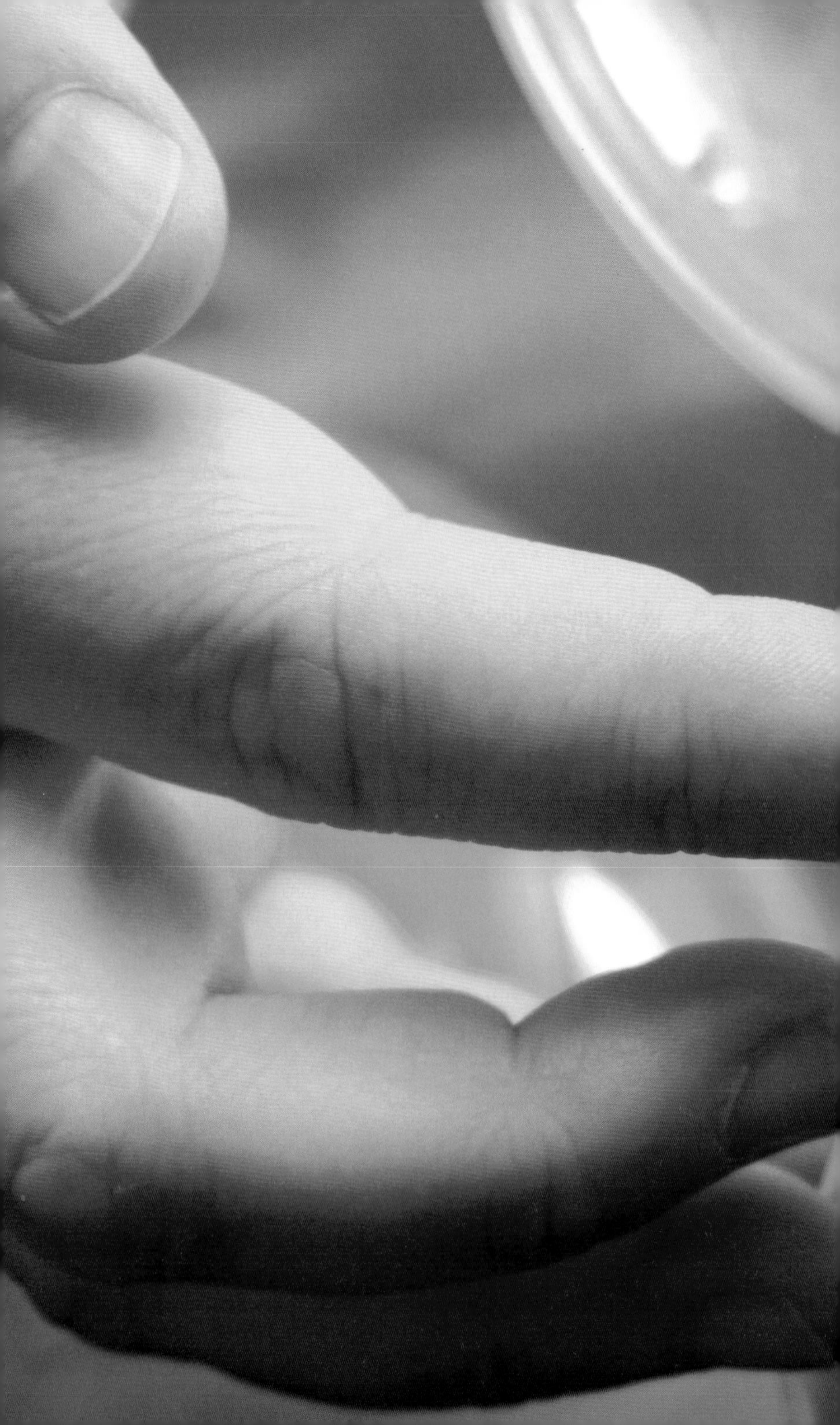

Part III

Enjoying Your Hamster

Chapter 9

Your Hamster's Behavior

Imagine that you are just five inches long, stand only two inches tall, and weigh only a few ounces. Imagine, too, that your natural instincts tell you that you should sleep all day, safely hidden in solitude within tunnels beneath the ground, and awaken in the evening to hunt for food under the cover of darkness.

Yet despite these powerful callings, you find yourself in a household of odd two-legged creatures who tower above you; who hoist you into the air, away from the safety of your beloved terra firma, often waking you from your peaceful day's slumber to do so. In other words, imagine yourself as a hamster and think about what life must be like. Viewed in this light, our world must be a pretty scary place for these tiny animals.

Hamster Highlights

But our world need not be, nor should it be, a frightening place for the hamster. In the right caretaker's hands, hamsters can be amazingly adaptable little creatures. We can use this characteristic to our mutual benefit: to make life more pleasant for the hamster and to make his care as simple as possible for us.

To create this win-win situation, you are wise to take the time to learn all that you can about this unique little creature, and then work to see our world through his eyes. You will learn that the hamster is more than willing to work with you in forging a mutually satisfying relationship.

You will also learn that stress can take a profound physical and emotional toll on this tiny animal. By looking at the world through his eyes, you can help prevent that life-threatening stress from gaining a foothold in your pet's life.

Imagine living in your world if you were as tiny as a hamster.

Form and Physique

If you were as tiny as a hamster, you can imagine that your physique would be a significant factor in how you behave and interact with the world.

Cheeks

Hamsters are famous for their puffy cheek pouches. The holding capacity of these pockets is such that they can double the size of the hamster's head when filled completely! The pouches enable the hamster to stow away food that he does not intend to eat immediately and that he would rather save for another time. He fills his cheek pouches with the excess food, then, when he returns to his home or chosen food hiding place, he empties his pouches by stroking his paws along his cheeks.

The cheek pouches also provide the hamster with an effective defense mechanism: When a hamster feels threatened, he can puff out his cheek pouches to make himself appear larger to enemies.

TIP

Tell the Kids

Make sure you warn your kids about the miracle that is the hamster cheek pouch. Think about it: The kids are happily watching their new pet nibble her breakfast one sunny morning. Then, suddenly, the new pet's face and head blow up like a balloon before their very eyes. Not a happy memory. Your job is to help make hamsterkeeping a positive experience for the kids, not an event that traumatizes them from the outset.

Teeth

As is the case with all rodents, a hamster's incisors will continue to grow throughout his life, primarily because these teeth have no roots. It is necessary, then, for hamsters to do a lot of gnawing—activity that will keep those ever-growing incisors sharp and at a manageable length. Needless to say, hamsters have very strong teeth and equally strong muscles associated with chewing, and you will have to be tolerant and accommodating of the gnawing behavior with which those traits are associated.

Legs

Where do hamsters get the strength for all that seemingly endless running on the wheel? Chalk it up to their muscular front legs. Stronger than the back legs, those front legs, in concert with his strong paws, enable the hamster not only to run, but also to burrow, climb, and wiggle himself out of precarious positions.

Eyes

Like many animals who are more active at night, hamsters have big eyes that seem to pop out at you when they turn their gaze your way. Their vision isn't perfect, however, because hamsters are farsighted. With his eyes positioned toward the side of his head (thus providing a greater angle of vision), your hamster is able to spot would-be predators in the distance and to his sides, so, with luck, he can escape with time to spare.

Your hamster's eyes, ears, nose, and whiskers tell him almost everything he needs to know about the world around him.

Ears

Your hamster can tell the difference between you and his other caretakers because of his extremely sensitive ears. He can typically hear sounds in extremely high frequencies. If you see your hamster flinch for some inexplicable reason, he may have simply heard a sound that you, with your comparatively inferior hearing, were not able to pick up.

Nose

The world of the hamster is defined by his acute sense of smell. Calling upon this tool, he can recognize his living environment, who his caretakers and enemies are, and when another hamster is sexually mature—all by the scents these important things in his life give off.

Hamsters also recognize other individual hamsters, because each carries a distinct scent (secreted by glands) that becomes familiar to them when they groom each other and nest together. If coexisting dwarf hamsters, for example, are separated temporarily or placed in completely different living quarters, it is very difficult for them to reestablish their bond peacefully—or at least without some heroic efforts on your part—because their scents may have changed.

Whiskers

Whiskers, or vibrissae, are the primary organs hamsters use to investigate their environment. Messages transmitted by his whiskers give the hamster his spatial sense and his ability to detect and navigate around objects blocking his path.

Will the Real Hamster Please Stand Up?

Most people you meet assume they understand hamsters. After all, what's to understand? They are quiet little rodents who eat, sleep, and sometimes run on a wheel. There's not much more to them, is there?

Well, as we have seen, there is much more, thank you very much. Let's explore the misconceptions people have about hamsters, because they provide much insight into the true hamster personality.

Misconception

Hamsters are easy-care pets and don't require much interaction with their owners.

Fact

Hamsters are easy-care pets, yes, but they also require attention from their owners. Goldens, in particular, thrive on it. Human interaction must be provided as part of a regular routine, not just when you remove the hamster from his cage once a week for the routine cleaning.

The conditions of the traditional golden hamster's native land—a barren landscape combined with a scarcity of food—are not conducive to sustaining large colonies of hamsters. The animals thus evolved into solitary creatures, forced by necessity to fend for themselves. They typically came together only to mate, the female then taking on the responsibility of raising her young on her own.

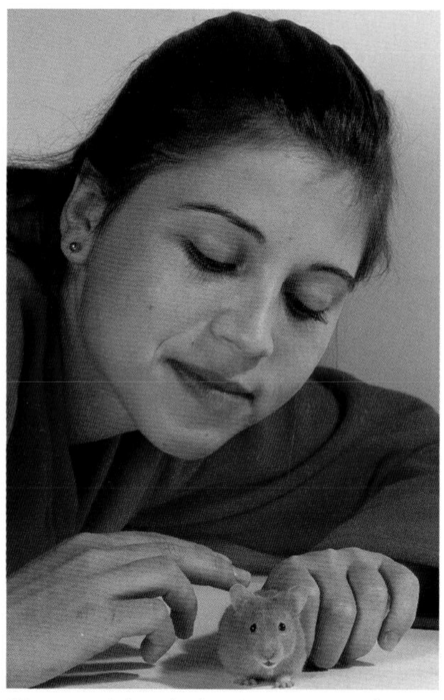

Hamsters need regular human attention or they will not thrive.

Assuming, incorrectly, that a single hamster is a lonely hamster, many owners ignore the natural solitary nature of these animals and insist on housing them together, usually with dire, and quite violent, results.

This is not the case, however, with the dwarfs. Although they can enjoy a certain level of human interaction and attention, they tend to be most content cohabitating and spending time with one or more of their own kind. You cannot, however, simply place a stranger into the domicile of a dwarf hamster who has already established his own turf. Introductions can be tricky (and not necessarily guaranteed), so if possible, try to purchase a pair of dwarf hamsters who have already bonded, either by birth or through the careful ministrations of an expert hamster handler.

Dwarfs may indeed be friendlier to their cage buddies than to the humans in their lives, and, in fact, regular interaction is a requirement for keeping dwarf hamsters tamed. Goldens, on the other hand, typically prefer the company of humans to that of their own kind. However, this bond takes time to develop and it cannot be forced.

Although he is a solitary creature at heart, the golden hamster must not simply be locked in a cage and ignored. He thrives on human care to help him adjust to life in captivity. In addition to cleanliness, a healthy diet, and a stress-free environment, he also needs play and regular human interaction.

The well-bred, well-socialized golden hamster who is properly housed, entertained, and cared for should be a gentle, sweet-natured animal. Do your job right and, in time, the hamster (any hamster, golden or dwarf) should come to know and trust you, and enjoy the time you spend together. Indeed, the bond that can form between a hamster and a human can be surprisingly deep.

Misconception

Hamsters are annoying. All they do is run endlessly on their wheels all night, keeping everyone awake with the squeaking.

Fact

Those who know and work with hamsters—pet owners, veterinarians, and animal welfare workers—know that far too many hamsters are bored and lonely, left in their cages with little or nothing to do. Hamsters can't bark like dogs to alert their owners to their frustration.

While dwarfs may have each other to play and interact with, the neglected golden has no choice but to languish within his cage, sleep more than he needs to, perhaps eat more than he should, and run endlessly on a squeaky wheel that is his only outlet for activity and stimulation. This animal would prefer to eat, sleep, burrow into the bedding of his enclosure, play with a variety of toys, and, yes, spend a bit of time each day interacting with the people in his family.

Misconception

Hamsters are nasty, difficult to socialize, and are prone to biting.

Fact

Depending on your pet's personality (and whether he is a golden or a dwarf), with proper, gradual, and gentle handling, he may choose to trust and respond to you and perhaps one or two other people. Or he may take a more openly social approach and embrace all humans who enter his realm. Either way, respect the animal for who he is and abide by what makes him most comfortable.

In return, your hamster will respect you and reward you with his own brand of hamster affection. So socialize your pet gently and gradually (as described in chapter 6) to a variety of well-behaved people and experiences at an early age, and establish a hamster routine. Allow him to nap peacefully and undisturbed during the day; and protect him from rough handling, loud voices and sounds, and household dangers. As a result of your efforts, you won't even be able to imagine the words "nasty" or "difficult" in connection with your little companion.

A hamster left alone in his cage all the time will become frustrated and bored.

Hamsters and Other Pets

While socialization, especially at a young age, is an important element in bringing up a healthy, well-adjusted hamster, this is best limited to just the humans in the hamster's life. While we may enjoy the vision of pets of all species coexisting in harmony and interacting happily with one another—dogs, cats, and all manner of other predators frolicking with tiny hamsters—this doesn't happen in the real world, and it shouldn't happen in your hamster's world either.

Yes, you may have seen a photograph of a large dog resting peacefully alongside an inquisitive hamster. But such a scene is staged and carefully supervised. And, even if the dog would never think of swallowing the hamster, just being near an obvious predator will only stress the hamster—a tiny prey animal, after all.

When you share your home with a variety of species, it is wise to respect the nature of each of those animals. Don't tease the cat by dangling a delectable hamster in her face, and don't stress the hamster by presenting him to the resident predator. The hamster will live just as happily—and probably longer—if he never interacts with other family pets.

The Great Escape Artist

Hamsters are consummate escape artists. Far too many hamster owners learn this the hard way. When owners compare hamster stories, you're likely to hear fantastic tales of hamster escapes and, hopefully, bizarre lost hamster recoveries. Understand this animal's propensity to run, take it seriously, and you can prevent your hamster from becoming the main character in such a story.

The escapes usually occur because of human error. The cage door is left open; the hamster is allowed to run unsupervised through the house; the hamster is housed in a wooden enclosure that proves no match for the animal's gnawing abilities; or perhaps a child is left to care for the animal when he or she is either too young for such a responsibility or uninterested in doing everything that needs to be done.

Sometimes the hamster takes advantage of a situation and creates his own escape route. He discovers a hole in the screen wall of his enclosure and works diligently to enlarge that hole. He discovers the latch on the door of his cage is broken and works all night long to spring it, or he chews through the plastic walls of his tube habitat. Or, perhaps during a foray outside his cage, he discovers an open door or a heating grate on the floor and cannot deny the calling to follow his insatiable curiosity.

Amazing Escapes

Many lost hamsters have been known to show up in the most unexpected, even shocking, places: toilets, sinks, outdoor trash cans, household furnaces, kitchen pantries, and beneath the cushions of the living room furniture (quite dangerous, especially if those are cushions of a reclining chair). Lose a hamster and be prepared to find him anywhere (if you are lucky enough to find him).

Stories abound of hamsters popping up, even up to a year after their disappearance, perhaps stealing sunflower seeds from the bird feeder, nonchalantly nibbling greenery in the vegetable garden, or exploring the folds and wrinkles of the sheets of his owner's bed.

The owner of such a refugee can't help but be amazed at how the hamster was able to sustain himself with food and water during his long walkabout—yet that owner must never lose sight of the fact that the animal's reappearance is nothing short of a miracle.

Survival Outdoors

When a hamster thought lost and gone forever is rediscovered, his owner may wonder how he was able to steer clear of the resident cats and other predators. This is especially true of the hamster who escapes into the great outdoors. Countless threats await this tiny animal, who has no experience surviving in our domestic neighborhoods. Yet many do survive, and while this is good for the hamster, it has broader repercussions for other wildlife within that ecosystem.

The hamster—the golden hamster in particular—is a desert native; he has not evolved among the various plant and animal species that we most often encounter in the typical Western Hemisphere neighborhood. His introduction to such an area will disturb the natural ecosystem and the food chain within that area.

A single lost hamster will probably cause little harm, but it's a different story if several people in a given area decide they no longer want their pets and "set

Your hamster is an accomplished escape artist. Prevent disaster by closely supervising all his out-of-cage adventures.

them free" in the wild. Aside from the ecological problems this can cause, tossing this tiny animal out to fend for himself is downright cruel. If, for any reason, you can no longer keep your pet, the kindest thing to do is find him a new and appropriate home or to take him to an animal shelter.

Preventing Escape

You can protect your hamster from becoming an escape statistic by monitoring him regularly when he is in his enclosure, and constantly when he is out and about playing. Examine his home daily for holes, gaps, and loose latches—anything the hamster may eventually use to escape—and, if you spot a problem, immediately make the necessary repairs or replace the habitat. Whenever your hamster is out of his cage, supervise him carefully and make sure he has no access to open doors or any escape routes. And finally, never leave your hamster in the care of someone who is not as diligent about your pet's supervision as you are.

Special Circumstances

Once you master the basics of hamster care and get to know your individual pet, you should encounter few problems in your relationship with this unique and enchanting animal. But circumstances may arise that test the routine you have established in caring for your pocket pet—circumstances to which you will both need to adjust.

A Long Winter's Nap

Let's say that an unexpected, unseasonable cold snap hits your area—so cold that the temperature inside your home takes a severe dip or perhaps causes your

How to Find a Hiding Hamster

It can happen to even the most diligent hamster keeper. You turn your back for one moment and your pet makes a run for it. Now what do you do? Act quickly, follow the steps below, and you may just find your little friend.

1. Secure the premises. Make sure doors, windows, and all portals of escape are locked down to prevent your loose hamster from making his way outdoors. Hide electrical cords that may attract a hamster who is in the mood to chew.
2. Lock up the predators. Round up resident dogs, cats, birds, and alligators, and confine them safely so that they do not end up "rescuing" the escapee.
3. Designate your search area. Determine which rooms are most likely hosting an escaped hamster. If the hamster escaped while you were playing with him in the family room, that is the logical place to begin your search. If he escaped from his cage without your knowledge, you will need to consider the entire house (and perhaps even all the great outdoors) your search area.
4. Start the hunt. Look in all dark spots and corners; use a flashlight if you need to. Carefully and gently inspect stacks of magazines, newspapers, and mail, as well as clothes in the laundry basket. Look under and inside sofa cushions, mattresses, and boxes of any sort. Use a flashlight to investigate the spaces under the stove and the refrigerator, and inspect each and every pantry shelf and kitchen cupboard.
5. Hamsters love to burrow, so consider any material, any location, any item that might in some way provide your pet with a cozy nest to be a likely hiding place.
6. Listen for scuffling and scratching noises.
7. Sprinkle morsels of your pet's favorite treats out in the open in the rooms in which you believe he may be hiding. The aroma might entice him to come out.
8. Find your hamster (we're thinking positively here). Find him perhaps snoozing peacefully in a cozy nest of his own making in the laundry room. Or find him nibbling happily on the treat "trap" you left in the middle of the living room.
9. Prevent this from ever happening again. Inspect your hamster's home for possible escape routes and provide your pet with a new house if you must. If your hamster escaped during playtime, tighten your own security measures to ensure that next time he won't be able to slip away.

It's not a good idea to let your hamster drift into a cold weather sleep. Avoid it by keeping him warm all the time.

power to go out for a couple of days. In the midst of this, you notice your hamster slowing down, sleeping more, and playing less.

Your hamster probably isn't ill. Rather, the cold temperatures are triggering the dormancy mechanism in his system. If nothing changes, the hamster will not hibernate in the classic sense, but he will eventually drift into a dormant sleep from which he can awake easily when it warms up.

It's not a good idea to allow your hamster to drift into this state. The animal may not be healthy enough to withstand the process physically, and it just isn't wise to keep him in temperatures lower than 65 degrees Fahrenheit. He is an indoor pet, pure and simple. If you notice that he is succumbing to a dormant state, gradually warm up his environment (in a safe way, of course, without direct heat or sunlight), and make sure he enjoys the winter wide awake and alert.

Going on Vacation?

There comes a time in all our lives when we must travel and leave our pets behind. Here, too, the hamster shines as an easy-care pet. He can be left alone for a weekend—a three-day weekend, maximum—as long as you leave him with all the comforts he will require.

Leave your pet an ample supply of food (more than you would feed for a single day), and make sure you leave only foods that won't spoil while you are away. To be safe, leave two bottles of fresh water on the side of the enclosure, rather than just one, in case one of the sipping tubes becomes clogged in your absence. (In this case, an open water dish simply will not do, because it can become soiled and/or spill so quickly.) Clean the enclosure and change the bedding, make sure the enclosure is in good repair and check all latches and locks, leave your pet a couple of his safest toys, and you're good to go.

> **TIP**
>
> **Find a Pet Sitter**
>
> To find an experienced, professional pet sitter in your area, check out the web sites of Pet Sitters International (www.petsit.com) and the National Association of Professional Pet Sitters (www.petsitters.org).

If you will be gone longer than two or three days, you need to make more detailed arrangements. You can ask a friend or neighbor to come in and clean the bedding, feed your hamster, and change the water, or contract with a pet sitter to care for your pet. If these options are not possible, you may even be able to take your pet to a boarding kennel. Pet hotels and veterinary boarding facilities frequently welcome small pets as well as dogs and cats.

On the Road with Hamsters

Don't discount the possibility of taking your pet with you. These small, quiet, odorless pets can make wonderful traveling companions, assuming they are well adjusted and comfortable with you. The key phrase here is "well adjusted." Timid, easily frightened animals will find travel stressful, and stress can lead to a variety of health and behavior problems.

If you do deem your hamster to be a good travel candidate and decide to take him with you, bring along a secure, escape-proof cage as your pet's home away from home (the plastic carrying-case models are ideal). Bring plenty of food, fresh bedding, and toys, and stick as closely as possible to your regular hamster care routine.

Just remind yourself that you must be even more diligent in supervising your pet than you are at home. When you arrive at your destination, don't allow unfamiliar people or animals to traumatize your pet. Keep to your normal routine, make sure the air temperature remains appropriate, allow your hamster his daytime naps, and you should enjoy a pleasant trip with your pet.

If you travel with your hamsters, be sure to take along some of their usual toys and tubes.

Hamster Smarts

Despite the fact that hamsters act mainly on instinct, they are very inquisitive, intelligent little critters if you give them the chance. They have the ability to retain new information through repetition. They can distinguish between their caretakers and strangers, thanks to their acute sense of smell and their ability to recognize voices. Your hamster also probably has a good memory whenever food is involved, evident when he returns to a cache where he has hidden food, or even to places or situations where he remembers receiving favored treats several days before.

Learning to Speak Hamster

One of the most enjoyable aspects of living with a hamster is the time you take playing with him and observing him in his daily routine. You will notice early on that your pet naturally engages in a variety of activities and expresses his emotions accordingly. A hamster who spends a great deal of time grooming himself, for example, washing his face and ears with his tiny paws, is showing you that he feels at home and is comfortable in his environment. You can also tell your hamster is relaxed when you see him stretching. At times you may even see him popping up into the air, expressing pleasure with a burst of energy.

When a hamster feels nervous or suspects danger, however, he may sit up on his haunches and sniff the air. If he starts walking with rigid legs and holds his stub of a tail straight up, it means that he is afraid of something. A reaction to a loud or abrupt noise may sometimes cause your hamster suddenly to start grooming himself for an extended time. Grooming helps the hamster focus on himself, which is a useful distraction from his fears. At the same time, he will most likely fold his ears back during the grooming as he attempts to discern the noise that startled him.

In time, your hamster will come to know you personally and look forward to his time with you.

Most vocalizations made by hamsters are to express aggression. When hamsters attack each other, you may hear the aggressor growling, hissing, chattering teeth, or making a muttering sound. The hamster in a defensive posture may screech to express fear.

The more time you spend with your hamster, the more you will understand his behaviors and activity patterns. He, in turn, will learn to recognize and respond to your scent, your tone of voice, and the daily routine you design for him. What fun it is to enter a room and hear a greeting from a hamster who not only knows and trusts you, but hopes you are there to spend some quality time with him outside of his cage. A hamster can bestow no greater honor on the people in his life.

Chapter 10

Having Fun with Your Hamster

As seasoned and dedicated hamster owners know, hamsters just want to have fun. These animals evolved to travel several miles a night in search of food, and therefore have a great deal of energy to expend. In the absence of vast deserts to traverse as part of their daily routine, toys and games are the ideal instruments for helping captive hamsters expend that energy and live long, happy, healthy lives.

As caretaker of this energetic creature, it's your job to make sure she pursues this grand mission as safely as possible. What an honor it is to know that the hamster, a species so dramatically different from our own, will often choose humans, even above her fellow hamsters, as her playmates. And how comforting to know that living up to that responsibility is relatively simple and fun.

Fun with Toys

Hamster fun and games revolve around toys. Contrary to popular belief, hamsters need far more than a wheel to keep themselves entertained and properly exercised. They thrive best with a variety of toys and games, many of which require your personal involvement. Manage the toys as you would the toys of a small child: Keep them in good repair and rotate them daily so that the hamster never has the opportunity to take her toys for granted. Then watch your small pet practically squeal in delight when you reintroduce toys that have been hidden away for a few days.

The Wheel

While the wheel can be abused with overuse, it's not necessary to deprive a hamster of this classic toy altogether. It should never be offered as the hamster's sole toy, however, nor should it be offered for hours and hours at a time.

A hamster who keeps her family up all night because she spends her every waking nighttime hour running on a wheel is a hamster who is not receiving the optimum care she deserves. By all means allow the hamster to partake of this favored hamster activity, but allow her to do so endlessly and you will find yourself with an exhausted, and possibly dehydrated, pet. Although it sounds silly, she may also become addicted to this particular toy, like a runner addicted to the adrenaline high, and so far there is no twelve-step program for animals afflicted with this particular compulsion.

Restricting your hamster's access to the wheel means placing the wheel within her habitat only when you wish her to play with it. In other words, don't leave it in the enclosure permanently. Offer your pet other diversions to occupy her time as well. Periodic, sporadic use will not only help to maintain your hamster's health, but also make the activity more of a treat for your pet, because it is not a constant in the animal's daily life. You may enhance the wheel experience for yourself by greasing it with petroleum jelly to keep the squeak under control.

When choosing a wheel for your hamster, make sure it is the right size for your particular pet. A dwarf hamster, for example, requires a smaller wheel than her larger golden cousin would need. Once you have chosen the appropriate wheel, keep it in good working order, spinning smoothly and free of exposed hardware and sharp edges. Finally, fill the remainder of your pet's playtime hours with other toys, offering her a broad spectrum of activities that will keep her healthy in both mind and body.

Don't let the hamster wheel become your pet's only diversion. She needs one-on-one attention from you.

The Ball

Another item that has become a favorite among hamsters and their owners is the so-called hamster ball. This is a clear plastic ball into which the hamster is placed so she can run as she would on the wheel. But

Safe Toys

The happiest hamsters have a large collection of toys, but they don't always know what is good—or safe—for them. It's your job to make sure the toys in your pet's collection meet your high standards of quality and safety. Follow these guidelines, and protect your small pet:

- Choose and create toys for your hamster that are made only of high-quality materials that are nontoxic and chew-safe.
- Inspect your hamster's toys regularly to ensure they are structurally safe and free of rough edges, sharp surfaces, and loose parts that could injure your pet.
- Avoid hamster toys with small parts or pieces that can break off or splinter and be swallowed, or cut your hamster's mouth and cheek pouches.

instead of remaining in one place, the hamster "rolls" the ball through the house, fully protected by the plastic shell that surrounds her.

Hamster balls come in a variety of sizes: smaller ones for dwarf hamsters, larger ones for goldens (placing a dwarf in a ball designed for a larger animal can be dangerous to the diminutive creature, so choose accordingly). The hamster ball is a safe, self-propelled vehicle that permits this small animal to explore the household without falling victim to a prowling cat, live electrical chords, or rocking chairs. Hamster balls provide a great deal of entertainment to a hamster, and can become an unexpected source of fascination and conversation for the hamster's owner. Owners tell, for instance, of hamsters who become so proficient in navigating these mobile toys that they chase resident cats through the hallways.

The hamster ball does not, however, relieve you of supervisory duty. Allow your pet to roll off unattended within her hamster ball and she may be stepped on by someone who doesn't realize she is out and about, or she may inadvertently escape and fall victim to everything the ball is designed to protect her from. Sadly, she may even be forgotten.

The hamster ball can also be overused. As with the wheel, to allow a hamster to overdo it with the ball, no matter how much she loves to use it and you love to watch her, is to invite exhaustion and dehydration, neither of which this tiny animal is physically equipped to tolerate. If you regard the hamster ball as an interactive toy, restrict your pet's use of it, keep the ball in good repair, and supervise your pet when she is inside it, it can be a productive, healthy toy that is as much fun for the hamster to "ride" as it is for you to watch.

Other Toys

The world can be your hamster's oyster with a steady stream of toys, reintroduced every few days to maintain the animal's interest. The items you collect for your pet's toy box can be a smorgasbord of commercially available toys designed especially for hamster play, as well as equally safe items you find around your own home.

Remember that the commercial tubes sold as housing (which are not necessarily the best housing choice; see chapter 4) can also make a wonderful playground for your hamster. Keep in mind, however, that many owners have seen their hamsters actually gnaw through the plastic of these tubes or have decided the tubes are too complicated to clean and reassemble regularly. Nevertheless, the tube setup can offer a hamster a great place for exercise and mental stimulation outside of her primary home enclosure.

Cardboard tubes make great hamster toys. You'll have to replace them as they get gnawed, though.

TIP

Keep safety in mind throughout the life of each toy. Periodically check everything for damage that could prove dangerous and even life-threatening to your hamster.

Use your imagination. You never know what might become a hamster's favorite toy. And always keep safety foremost in your mind. Both structure and material are significant when you are making, evaluating, or buying hamster toys. Make sure your pet's toys are made of materials that are nontoxic, structurally safe, and cannot be easily destroyed by gnawing. Check that there are no small pieces that can break off and be swallowed. In time, evaluating hamster toys will become second nature to you.

Homemade Toys for Hamsters

A great way to save money and get creative is to make toys at home for your hamster. Of course, nothing should have sharp edges or contain toxic substances and materials. Just think about what you might include or avoid as a toy for a baby, and follow that example. For instance, you never want to offer your pet items made of materials that might suffocate or injure her, such as plastic grocery bags or staples.

In this spirit, the following are several ideas for safe homemade hamster toys:

- Paper bags
- Shoe boxes
- PVC tubes
- Toilet paper and paper towel rolls
- Facial tissue boxes
- Wrapping paper rolls
- Cardboard oatmeal canisters

Now that you have the supplies, it is time to use your imagination. As we have learned, hamsters love to explore their surroundings. You can satisfy this passion by creating mazes out of empty cardboard rolls and boxes. Use nontoxic glue to connect the ends of the rolls and boxes, and be sure the maze tunnels are wide enough for your hamster to fit through comfortably.

Another great toy for climbing and hiding can be made of facial tissue boxes with holes of various sizes cut into the sides. You can glue the boxes together (again, nontoxic glue only, please) and stack them on top of each other or place them side by side. The possibilities are many and, keeping safety in mind at all times, this presents a great way for you to get creative, as well as to involve your kids in the fun.

Remember that your hamster will eventually gnaw through anything made of cardboard, so be sure to check and replace the parts of your hamster playground regularly and frequently.

Out and About

Although many a hamster enjoys playing with various types of toys within the secure confines of her enclosure, she may also relish the opportunity to leave her happy home from time to time and explore the world beyond the cage door. Don't even think of trying this until your hamster has adjusted completely to her new home and to her human family members. Then, once you have gained her trust, you can help broaden her horizons beyond the cage doors.

Needless to say, granting the common hamster wish of exploring the great beyond can be dangerous if the basic tenets of safety and decorum are not met each and every time your pet is allowed to roam. First, the room in which the hamster will wander freely must be made hamster-safe *before* the animal is allowed out to explore. Look around—get down on the floor—and try to see the world through your hamster's eyes. Evaluate what might be irresistibly interesting and physically dangerous. Then prepare accordingly. For example, floor heating vents must be covered; all doors and windows must be closed, including cabinet doors; pet dogs, cats, and other animals should be safely confined in

Everyone in the house must know when the hamster is out and about, because one misstep could be fatal.

> **TIP**
>
> Keep in mind that if you have dwarf hamsters, you must be even more vigilant with loose pets. Never forget that the tiny dwarfs are fast, curious, impetuous, and very active. They require even more of your attention and forethought in determining what items and situations could prove dangerous to their wily ideas.

another room; those delectable electrical cords must be safely moved out of the hamster's line of vision and access; and virtually anything that might attract the attention of this inquisitive animal and cause her harm should be removed. One mistake, a one-time deviation from these rules of conduct and preparation, and your pet hamster could be gone forever.

Once you have secured the premises, alert the family that there will soon be a hamster on the loose and everyone must thus mind their manners and walk with their eyes to the ground. This is not the time to start a rousing game of indoor touch football, to invite the neighborhood kids in for a 5-year-old's birthday party, or to permit the family dog to play chase through the halls with the family cat. In other words, the house is on high alert until the hamster is safe once more within her happy home.

Rather than allowing the hamster free run of a given room in the house, a safer option is to establish a play area for your pet outside of her habitat—a playpen, if you will—in which she can enjoy being out while still having the

A fall from a table can kill a hamster. Remember that they are fast critters, and don't let them roam where they can get hurt.

Caution! Hamsters Roaming

The world can be a dangerous place for a hamster who is allowed to run free—a fact that this tiny animal may not recognize. Here are some common household dangers that can threaten a hamster, even when she is being supervised by a vigilant owner.

- Open doors can slam suddenly, catching and squashing your tiny, unsuspecting pet.
- Small, pointed objects can tear cheek pouches if the hamster attempts to store them in her cheeks.
- Overexposure to the sun can cause heatstroke.
- Watch for nibbling. Some plants are poisonous, often fatal, when ingested by a hamster who doesn't know better.
- Be on your toes! You can step on your hamster if she is not being watched carefully. And play watchdog for other people, too, who may walk in and not realize that a tiny hamster is running about.
- Ventilation grates provide the perfect avenue for escape, and far too many adults have sad stories about hamsters from their childhood who escaped just that way. Obviously, the guilt and loss don't easily dissipate. Prevention is the best medicine.
- Hamster toys in disrepair or made of materials that are dangerous or toxic to these small pets should be discarded right away.
- Hot objects and appliances (toasters and curling irons come to mind) can cause serious burns. You don't allow your children near these items; keep your hamsters away, too.
- The kitchen is filled with accidents waiting to happen. This is not a place to let a hamster play.
- Fumes from wood stains, varnishes, cleaning agents, and other household chemicals can damage a hamster's fragile respiratory system, and the materials themselves can be deadly to the animal if ingested.
- Doors to cupboards, drawers, the refrigerator, the freezer, the dishwasher can all clamp shut on a hamster cleverly hidden inside, and the little guy just may suffocate (or never be found, until it's too late).
- Remember that curiosity can kill the hamster.

same level of safety and security. As we have seen, the plastic tube housing setup provides such a play area, but you can also build a makeshift enclosure of your own with temporary wall boundaries—perhaps a child's wading pool or a large plastic storage box.

Furnish the playpen with your pet's favorite toys. Then sit back and enjoy the view as she explores her new environment, the new sights and sounds, and the new objects in her path. When you establish a play area, however, you must not leave the hamster unsupervised; *she must be supervised at all times during her forays out of her habitat.* Never underestimate your hamster's abilities as an escape artist—abilities that can be even more effective in a low-security, temporary enclosure or in those moments when she is granted liberty from her humble abode.

Sharing the Joy of Hamsters

Do you love hamsters so much that you just can't keep it to yourself? There are opportunities that link hamster owners together so they can share their mutual affection for, and fascination with, these animals. Meeting others who share your passion makes hamsterkeeping even more enjoyable and rewarding.

Show-and-Tell

Because hamsters are often members of households with children, it is inevitable that one day one of the kids will want to take the family's pet hamster to school for show-and-tell. This not only provides a unique and, we would hope, pleasant outing for the animal (leave the more timid hamster at home), but it also gives children the opportunity to educate their peers about proper hamsterkeeping. Given the number of hamsters in our world who do not receive optimum care, your child can do the species a great service in this role as hamster educator.

Taking the family pet to school can be a source of great pride for a child, but it's best that kids do not do this alone. The trip should be supervised by a parent (or a teacher well versed in hamster care) to prevent accidents, escapes, or similar tragedies. For the hamster's health and safety, she should not be passed around to everyone in the class, nor should she be allowed to meander around on Jimmy's best friend's desk. Losing a hamster at school, or seeing her fatally injured from an accident, is not a childhood memory anyone needs to carry into adulthood.

A visit to a classroom by a healthy hamster who enjoys the best of care and consideration, however, can be a memorable experience for all involved. The hamster should be transported to the class the same way she is transported anywhere (to the veterinarian, grandma's house, and so on): in a safe, secure travel cage, fully equipped with bedding, food, water, toys, and hiding places. This not only ensures her safety, but also alleviates any potential stress she may experience being away from her home.

A pet hamster can be a source of great pride for a youngster.

As the members of the class "ooh" and "ahh" over the adorable, sweet-faced pocket pet in their midst, the animal's young owner can tell the class all about the nutrition, attention, housing, and health care required to keep a hamster healthy and as long-lived as possible. Perhaps the other kids will take some of that information home to their own families and to their own hamsters. It's an interchange where everyone wins, and all because a child wishes to share a love for hamsters.

Hamster Shows

You have no doubt heard of dog shows, horse shows, and cat shows. Well, believe it or not, hamsters are exhibited at shows, as well.

Typically sponsored by local and national hamster clubs, shows may be held as individual events, or they may be incorporated into other similar exhibitions, such as rat and mouse shows, county fairs, or pet shows that showcase all species of companion animals. They are run very much as are shows for other species, with specified classes for the entrants (in this case, classes for the different coat and color varieties). The winners of these classes then typically move up to compete with increasingly smaller groups of entrants until one hamster is finally proclaimed Best in Show.

The hamsters are usually displayed anonymously in show cages, the cage styles typically designated by the club sponsoring the show to promote fairness. The animals within those cages are judged on their color, structure, hair quality, and temperament. They don't need to prance around a show ring or show off their ability to jump fences; they just need to look cute, well groomed, and well bred.

It's fun to go to hamster shows to see the fancy hamsters and to meet veteran breeders.

Show hamsters are not usually average pet hamsters—unless the show includes pet classes. The more traditional show hamsters tend to be the products of dedicated breeders who have added breeding and showing to their list of enjoyable hamster pursuits.

It's nice to meet these veteran hamster lovers at a show, especially if you hope one day to show your hamster. The wise veteran will welcome newcomers to the fold and share with them their knowledge and perhaps even sell them some of their show stock. Only by bringing new blood—and new hamsters—into the world of hamster showing will the activity have a chance of gaining popularity and carrying on into future generations.

If you are interested in going to a hamster show, contact local veterinarians who treat hamsters and check the Internet for hamster or other pet rodent clubs in your area for information on upcoming shows. You can also contact those in charge of the various fairs in your city, county, and state to see if hamsters will be some of the animals on display at these events. Check out the appendix in this book, as well, for hamster web sites through which you might be able to contact like-minded hamster lovers who may know about show activities in your area.

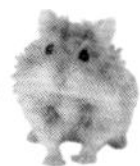

Appendix

Learning More About Your Hamster

A Few Good Books

Bucsis, Gary, and Barbara Somerville, *Training Your Pet Hamster*, Barron's Educational Series, 2005.

Logsdail, Chris, Peter Logsdail, and Kate Hovers, *Hamsterlopaedia: A Complete Guide to Hamster Care*, Ringpress Books, 2004.

Starosta, Paul, *Face-to-Face with the Hamster*, Charlesbridge Publishing, 2004.

Vanderlip, Sharon L., DVM, *Dwarf Hamsters*, Barron's Educational Series, 1999.

Stories About Hamsters

Baglio, Ben M., *Hamster Hotel*, Scholastic, 1999.

Banks, Lynne Reid, *I, Houdini: The Autobiography of a Self-Educated Hamster*, Econo-Clad Books, 1999.

Ryan-Lush, Geraldine, *Malcolm and the Hamster Lady*, Mulberry Books, 2005.

White, Lauren, *Hamtaro: Little Hamsters, Big Adventures*, Viz Video, 2002.

Wiebe, Trina, *Hamsters Don't Glow in the Dark*, Rebound by Sagebrush, 2003.

Magazines

Critters USA
P.O. Box 6050
Mission Viejo, CA 92690
(949) 855-8822
www.animalnetwork.com
An annual magazine for owners of small pets.

Hamsters
P.O. Box 6050
Mission Viejo, CA 92690
(949) 855-8822
www.animalnetwork.com
An annual magazine for hamster owners; part of the "Popular Critters" series.

On the Internet

The Internet offers hamster owners another place to find information on hamster care, as well as to get to know hamster enthusiasts all over the world. This high-tech-hamster network includes bulletin boards, veterinary advice forums, and information on everything from the nuances of hamster care to special problems to behavior to breeding.

Here are some useful web sites that have educational information on hamsters (both goldens and dwarfs), including facts on care, showing your pet, behavioral information, and fun things you can do with your hamster.

All About Dwarf Hamsters
http://russiandwarfhamsters.tripod.com/
Everything you ever wanted to know about dwarf hamsters.

Hamster Central
www.hamstercentral.com
Everything you ever wanted to know about hamsters.

Hamster Heaven
www.hamster-heaven.com
A site dedicated to all aspects of hamster care.

Hamsterific
www.hamsterific.com
A site dedicated to all aspects of hamster care.

Internet Hamster Association of North America
http://groups.msn.com/InternetHamsterAssoc
An excellent network resource for hamster information and links.

The National Hamster Council
www.hamsters-uk.org
The home page of a longtime hamster organization in the United Kingdom. You'll find links to other organizations worldwide.

Index

Photo Credits

Tammy Raabe Rao, Rubicat Photography: 1, 4–5, 8–9, 11, 12, 14, 16, 19, 22, 24, 27, 28, 30, 31, 35, 38, 41, 43, 46, 48, 51, 52, 53, 54, 59, 60, 61, 62, 67, 73, 76, 77, 79, 81, 83, 84, 85, 88, 90, 93, 94–95, 96, 97, 98, 101, 104, 106, 109, 110, 111, 113, 115, 116, 119, 120

Isabelle Francais: 18, 21, 32, 36–37, 40, 50, 57, 68, 69, 71, 92, 100, 108